Courts and Trials

LAW IN ACTION SERIES
Second Edition for Teachers

RIEKES–ACKERLY
LESSONS IN LAW FOR
YOUNG PEOPLE

WEST PUBLISHING COMPANY
St. Paul   New York   Los Angeles   San Francisco

ACKNOWLEDGEMENTS

The people who helped us through the years in developing and refining the *Law in Action Series* are too numerous to give each of them the credit they deserve here. The teachers, administrators, students, parents, juvenile court personnel and law-related resource people each require a personal thank you.

We would like to say a special word of appreciation to Dr. Isidore Starr who has been a constant source of inspiration and guidance to us. Mary Curd has given excellent assistance in many facets of the revision. Trudy Faust has been invaluable as an editor and researcher. Susan Spiegel has provided legal help and guidance without which we could not have met our deadline. To Mary Engelbreit, who created many of the illustrations, thank you for your talent, skill, cooperation, and perceptiveness.

The responses of students to the material have been extremely valuable in revising *Courts and Trials* for this Second Edition. Their overwhelming interest, frankness, and eagerness to learn about the law continues to make our endeavors worthwhile.

To our husbands, Richard Ackerly and Andrew Trivers and our parents, Dr. and Mrs. George Mahe and Mr. and Mrs. Max Riekes, who were always supporting us with encouraging helpful suggestions, very special thanks.

To everyone at West Publishing Company thanks for unfailing patience, understanding, and support.

Linda Riekes
Sally Mahe Ackerly

1 Students will begin to analyze origins of conflicts and to find alternative ways of resolving conflicts.

2 Students will understand that the U.S. judicial system is a legal way of resolving conflicts.

3 Students will learn the function and operation of the judicial system with emphasis on the concept of due process.

4 Students will begin to understand that the responsibility for an efficient and just judicial system depends on active citizen participation.

5 Students will develop questioning and critical thinking skills by preparing for and participating in their own mock trial.

Students:

This book is about ways of resolving conflicts. Everyone experiences conflicts. Sometimes conflicts involve the law, sometimes they don't. This book can help you improve your skill in handling conflicts in your own life. Whether or not the conflicts you have involve the law, we believe it is important for you to learn how conflicts occur and how better to resolve them when they do happen.

This book will also show you how the court system in the United States handles legal conflicts between people. There are laws that set down certain steps or procedures the courts must follow when deciding a case. The purpose of these procedures is to resolve legal problems fairly.

To understand more about how courts work you need to learn the responsibilities of the people who work in the courts. You also need to learn the vital part witnesses, jurors, and citizens have in the court system. Putting on your own mock trial will give you first hand information about how the courts work.

We believe that the best way to gain skill in resolving conflicts and knowledge of the judicial system is to become actively involved in these lessons. We hope you can help others learn what you have learned.

Sincerely,
Linda Riekes
Sally Mahe Ackerly

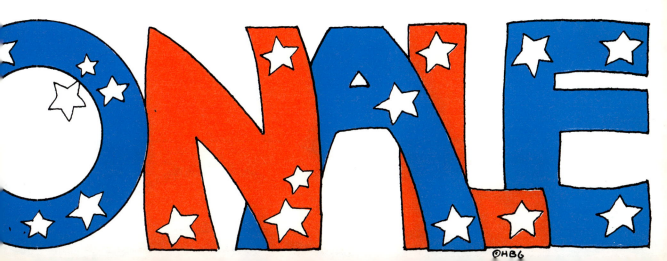

TABLE OF CONTENTS

PAGE

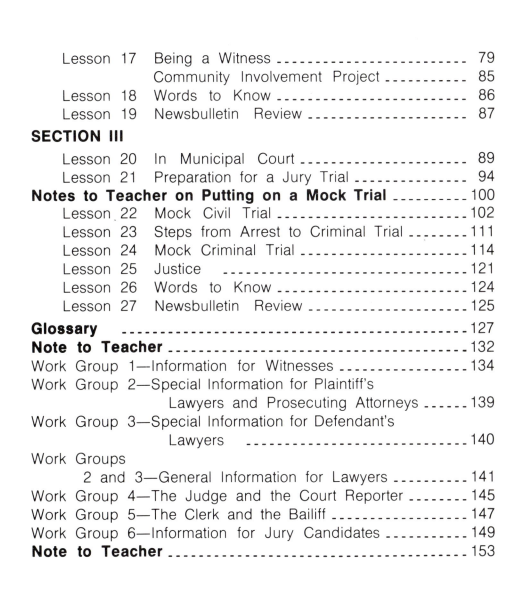

General Note to Teacher:

Field Trips

A field trip to a court building needs to be extremely well thought out to see if it is both feasible and profitable for your particular class. Considerations should include:

    a) what kind of trial;

    b) what is the best day to go (Monday could be Voir Dire and by Friday there may not be any trials);

    c) when are courts in recess;

    d) whether you can interview any court personnel;

    e) whether you can learn anything about the trial from a court official before you plan your trip.

Before going to a court, students should understand the difference between real and TV trials. They should know that they will see only a portion of a trial or may not even be able to see a trial at all. The trial might be postponed for any number of reasons, including illness of a witness. The trial might be settled moments before it is scheduled to begin or moments after it begins. Students should also be aware that they may have to sit quietly through some very dry testimony or they may not be able to hear witnesses clearly.

We recommend that a field trip to a court not be taken until after you have completed Lesson 17 so that students understand judicial procedure. It will have more meaning for them if they have studied conflict resolution, appeal procedures, responsibilities of court personnel as well as other lessons in *Courts and Trials*, Second Edition. The field trip can be a very helpful way of reinforcing learning from the lessons about court procedure as well as teaching new information and motivating students for their mock trial.

Community Involvement Projects

There are Community Involvement Projects interspersed throughout this unit. The purpose of these activities is to give students the chance to put to use in their community something they have learned in the classroom. The purpose of involving students in these projects is to develop the skill of seeing another's need and reaching out in a responsible way to fulfill that need. These projects can take more time to plan than regular classroom lessons. However, some may be facilitated by outside helpers, such as parents, police officers, law students, or volunteers. These projects can be looked upon as "suggested activities." Some may prove to be a jumping-off point for a long-range project undertaken by the class.

Newsbulletin Reviews

Periodic testing on information presented in the lessons can be done by using the "Newsbulletin Reviews." There is a Newsbulletin Review after each major section. Our purpose in providing this technique was not only to test the students' grasp of information, but also to stimulate interest and motivate students to respond as fully as possible. Also, the newsbulletins have been used as an effective means of communication between classroom and school administration and community.

To transform the "test" into a newsbulletin requires extra typing work. Instructions for how to accomplish this transformation are given in the Newsbulletin Review lessons and a model finished newsbulletin is given on page 45.

Resource Persons

Since providing resource persons and field trips requires planning, we wanted to bring this to your attention at the beginning. Appropriate places to bring in resource persons, such as lawyers, law students and court personnel, are on pages 69, 73, 113, 132 and 133.

On these pages you will find specific ideas on how to make effective use of a resource person in the classroom. Experience has shown us that if the resource person and the students focus on a topic or activity, the tendency of a resource person to talk "at" the students is lessened.

SECTION I
DECISIONS AND CONFLICTS

Objective: **Students will be able to analyze what causes conflicts between people.**

The picture below shows some conflicts. A  is usually a problem between at least two people.*

Can you tell what each of these conflicts is about? What you do think caused each conflict?

*However, a person may also have a problem (conflict) within himself/herself.

Conficts between people, groups of people, and between countries arise all the time.

Sometimes conflicts arise because people want the same thing.
Sometimes they arise because of the decisions people make to
do things.

A. Write down three things

really want to do today:

1. _____

2. _____

3. _____

B. Make up possible conflicts that
    might occur because of your
    three decisions:

1. _____
    _____
    _____
    _____

2. _____
    _____
    _____
    _____

3. _____
    _____
    _____

Note to teacher: You might have several students list on the
chalkboard what they really wanted to do today in one column
and then in the column next to it, what possible conflicts might
occur from their decision, then discuss.

Some examples students give are: riding their bikes to
school—possible conflict with school rules; not going to
school—possible conflict with state law, etc.

Do any of your decisions concern only yourself and have no
effect on anyone else? Please explain.

Conflicts sometimes occur because people don't think carefully about how their actions affect other people.

This man decided to sing in the shower at 3 a. m.

What conflict situations might arise because of his actions?

Since everyone experiences conflicts it is important for everyone to know different ways of resolving conflicts.

RESOLVING CONFLICTS

Objective: **Students will discuss at least four alternative ways of resolving conflict.**

Students will discuss with one another the need for having a fair way to settle conflicts between people.

These men are using one way to resolve conflict. They decided to settle a conflict by dueling with guns.

Can you think of other ways people have tried to settle conflicts in the past?

There are alternatives to violence and fighting for settling conflicts.

Here are some alternatives people use to resolve conflicts. People may need to try more than one of these ways, or think of other ways to handle their problems.

1.   Talking about the conflict

2.   Working out a compromise

3.   Chance

4.   Going to someone and asking them to decide

What other ways are there to resolve conflicts?

The following stories are examples of conflicts that come up between people. Working alone, write down how you would resolve each of these conflicts. After you have decided how best to resolve these conflicts, discuss the questions on page 8.

1. "I want to sharpen my pencil whenever I want to."

"We can't hear what is going on in class with the pencil sharpener going."

How would you resolve this conflict?

2. "I turned the corner on a green light and you hit my car."

"Your light was yellow and your car plowed into mine."

How would you resolve this conflict?

3.

"I want to talk to my friends while we watch this movie."

How would you resolve this conflict?

"If you are talking, I can't hear the movie."

4. "I found that dollar on the floor. It's mine."

"But I lost a dollar in this room this morning. It's mine!"

How would you re-solve this conflict?

5.

How would you re-solve this conflict?

QUESTIONS TO DISCUSS

1. Explain your suggestions for resolving the conflicts on the previous pages. Be certain to include the reasons you have for thinking this will work. Then, based on the reasons given, the class could vote on the best way to resolve each conflict.

2. Do you think it really makes a difference if the way the conflict is resolved is fair? Why wouldn't any way be good as long as it stopped the conflict?

3. Think of a conflict you have had recently, perhaps with a brother, sister or friend. What was the conflict about? What did you do to try to resolve it? Would you try the same way of resolving it again?

4. These women have a conflict. Can you think of any way the conflict can be resolved so that both women will be happy?

Conflicts can't always be resolved so that everyone is happy.

Sometimes no one is really happy with the solution to a conflict. Can you think of any other types of conflicts which can not be resolved so that everyone is happy?

When people can't resolve conflicts by themselves and their problem involves the law, they may go to the courts. Courts are intended to provide a legal, orderly, and fair way to resolve disputes between people.

INTRODUCTION TO COURTS

Objective: Students will be able to recognize that courts can resolve some conflicts which people are unable to settle themselves.

Students will be able to recognize the differences between civil and criminal cases.

Students will be able to explain how the authority of the courts can affect their lives.

People use courts to resolve certain conflicts when other alternatives have been tried and have not worked or when the conflicts involve criminal acts. The court system makes up one branch of government, called the judicial branch. It has authority to settle conflicts within society. Many different kinds of conflicts are resolved through the courts. Look at the pictures on pages 9 and 10. Find some of the different kinds of problems the courts handle.

Most of the problems handled by the courts can be divided into two groups.

CIVIL CASES

involve conflicts over private rights of individuals or groups.

One person or group takes legal action against another person or group. (For example: a person or group seeks money damages for an injury by another person or group; a person or group seeks to require another person or group to fulfill the terms of a contract.)

Which of the problems in the pictures on pages 9 and 10 would you

as civil cases?

Why?

CRIMINAL CASES

involve violations of criminal laws which local, state, or federal governments have enacted. (Violating a law is breaking that law.)

The city, state, or federal government takes legal action against a person accused of a crime.

Which of the problems in the pictures on pages 9 and 10 would you

as criminal cases?

Why?

Note to teacher:

Civil

1. Inheritance
2. Family problems
3. Personal injuries and property damage
4. Consumer disputes
5. Discrimination in employment
6. Fight**
7. Violations of air pollution laws*

Criminal

1. Armed robbery
2. Traffic violation
3. Fight**
4. Violations of air pollution laws*
5. Juvenile offenses

*It is very difficult to make a clear distinction between civil and criminal cases of this kind. The U.S. government, for example, could sue a corporation for damages (a civil action). This extends the definition given for civil cases between two private parties.

**A case could be both civil and criminal. If a person hits another person, it can be both a criminal act and the basis for a civil suit for damages.

What Can The Courts Do?

Act out the following scenes. Have different people play the parts in Scene I, Scene II, and Scene III.

SCENE I:

"I don't care; let them sue me. What will happen?"

SCENE II:

"So what! One more traffic ticket here or there."

SCENE III:

"What can the landlord do anyway if I don't pay my rent?"

"You could lose your case and pay a fine."

"The court could force you to pay a fine—take away your driver's license."

"You could be evicted (put out of your home) by the court."

SCENE I:
"I didn't know that!"

SCENE II:
"I didn't know that!"

SCENE III:
"I didn't know that!"

"The court has power to enforce the laws. It can decide civil cases and evict people or force them to pay damages or to keep contract promises. It can try criminal cases and punish people who break the law by giving them fines or prison sentences."

Courts have the power to take a person's property, freedom, and even his/her life. They have the power to settle conflicts between people. Their decisions might result in a person losing a home; parents losing custody of their children; businesses being forced to pay fines or completely change a practice. The power of the courts can directly affect your life.

Now—make up your own scene about someone who didn't realize the power of the courts. Write a dialogue of what each person would say. Choose another classmate to take the other part, and present your scene to the class.

Your Scene.

THE COURT SYSTEM

Objective: **Students will be able to describe how the court system is set up.**

Students will be able to identify the kinds of cases handled by each type of court.

There are two court systems: state and federal. The state court system includes several kinds of courts at the county and city level.

The different courts within the state court system have authority to hear and resolve only cases involving certain subject matter or laws as set out in the state constitution and statutes or by state supreme court rule. The authority given a court to hear certain cases is known as the court's JURISDICTION.

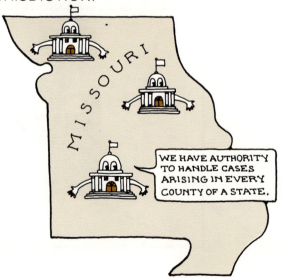

WE HAVE AUTHORITY TO HANDLE CASES ARISING IN EVERY COUNTY OF A STATE.

Be a Detective.

Search the next three pages to find out which
courts would handle the following cases.

1. Joe, 15 years old, was accused of stealing hubcaps. His
   case will be handled in the_____. Juvenile
   Court.

2. Guy was accused of robbery. His case will be handled in
   the _____. Criminal Trial Court.

3. Federal narcotics officers arrested George S., a drug smug-
   gler, for bringing narcotics into the U.S. by boat. George is
   accused of breaking a federal law; his case will be handled
   in the _____. U.S. District Court.

4. Marlene, owner of an apartment building, is suing Joe's Tree
   Service because a tree Joe was cutting down fell on the
   apartment building and caused serious damage. Marlene is
   suing Joe's Tree Service for $5,000.00. Her case will be
   handled in the _____. Civil Trial Court.

5. Doris and Bill have been married fifteen years. They want a
   divorce. Their case will be handled in the _____.
   Domestic Relations Court.

6. When Mr. Allen died a will was found which left most of his
   money to charities. His only daughter, Greta, believes that
   she should get more of his estate. Her case will be
   handled in _____. Probate Court.

7. Georgia Fernandez feels that the dry cleaner ruined her new
   coat. The dry cleaner says no. She wants one hundred
   dollars for her coat from the dry cleaning company. Her
   case will be handled in _____. Small Claims Court.

Note to teacher: For more work with types of courts, you might
have students make up cases of their own and ask other students
to tell in which courts their cases would be handled.

Note to student: The courts in your state may have different names than those given here. For example, the general trial level courts may be known as circuit courts, district courts, superior courts, or something else. The appeals courts may be known as courts of appeals, superior courts (appellate division), or something else. Even the highest state court may not always be called the "supreme court." You could check with a lawyer or court officer to find out what the various types of courts in your state are commonly called.

Other State Courts
In many states there are magistrate courts and small claims courts.

magistrate court

handles cases involving minor civil lawsuits and minor criminal offenses.

small claims court

handles cases involving minor disputes, usually about business or contractual agreements, where the damages asked for are less than $1000. People can represent themselves in small claims court.

"You owe me $200.00 for breaking my tooth."

"It wasn't my fault. I owe you nothing."

"The wallpaper your company put up peeled off the next day. I refuse to pay my bill."

"You owe us our fee. We put up the wallpaper according to our agreement."

Note to teacher: Magistrate courts (which may also be called county courts) are courts of *limited jurisdiction*. That generally means that these courts can only hear cases involving an amount of money lower than a set statutory amount. In rural areas, the courts of limited jurisdiction are often called justice of peace courts. Some states do not have small claims courts which are separate from the courts of limited jurisdiction; instead all claims under a certain amount can be heard in the same court and either party can be represented by a lawyer. In separately constituted small claims courts, there are often special restrictions on the use of the courts. These may include a prohibition of representation by lawyers and a limitation on the number of times a person can sue in the courts. These restrictions are aimed at preventing the small claims court from being routinely used by companies for debt collection. For more detail on small claims court see *Young Consumers*, Second Edition, Law in Action Series, West Publishing Company.

Federal Court System

1. Read the newspaper for one week. Try to find:

   > one article on a conflict handled
   >   by a local court;
   >
   > one article on a conflict handled
   >   by the State Supreme Court;
   >
   > on article on a conflict handled
   >   by a federal court or the U.S.
   >   Supreme Court

   Make certain that you write the date and the newspaper's
   name on the article. (That information is the source of the
   article.) Then take all of the articles and, as a class, make a
   "Week at the Courts" bulletin board. Analyze the articles and
   include a one-page report, explaining what happened in the
   courts that week. Add this report to your bulletin board.
   Your bulletin board and attached report will help other people
   see all the different kinds of cases that the courts handle in
   the United States and in your particular area.

2. Make a map showing where the courts are located in your
   community. Begin by getting a map of your city or county.
   You might make your own by copying one. Then look up
   the addresses of city or county, state and federal courts in the
   telephone book. Locate these courts on your map. Place
   the name of the court, its address and phone number on your
   map. Your class might also add a drawing or picture of
   each building.

   You might share your map with your family and even with
   people in the courts. If you want to make a more detailed
   map you could add information on what each court does.

WHAT IS FAIR COURT PROCEDURE?

Objective: **Students will compare court procedures at different times in history and recognize the development of court procedures throughout history**

Students will be able to identify basic elements of fair treatment people should expect in court.

PROCEDURE

is a series of steps or rules to be followed.

Throughout history, different types of court procedures have been used to settle conflicts that arise between people. Ideas about what are fair ways or fair procedures to use to handle conflicts have changed with the times and are still changing. Below is a criminal case about a man who broke the law by killing two people. Read how courts at different times in history handled this case. After reading how each court handled the case, decide what was fair and what was unfair about each court procedure from your own point of view. Be able to explain the reasons for your decision.

THE CASE

A man and a woman were married. The married woman fell in love with another man and ran away from her husband. The husband chased the couple and killed both of them.

Note to teacher: This lesson asks students to decide what was fair or unfair in trials in cultures and historical periods different from their own. For the purpose of the lesson, we feel students should be encouraged to base their decisions on their point of view now rather than basing a decision on what they might have decided if they were living at the time these trials took place.

1.   A TRIBE'S COURT—1000 B.C.

Ola, the oldest man in the tribe, was the judge.   A tribesman brought Mo to him saying that Mo had killed two people.   The judge had known Mo since he was a baby and he decided that Mo should not be punished for what he had done.

From your point of view:

Was there anything fair about this court trial?

Was there anything unfair about this court trial?

2.   AN ANCIENT COURT—1 B.C.

Quintus Tiber was appointed governor and judge of Judea by the Emperor in Rome.   A villager in Judea named Mo was brought before Tiber and charged with the murder of two people.   Tiber asked Mo to tell his side of the story.   Tiber also heard the stories of many witnesses.   Tiber didn't know very much about Mo or the customs of the people in this land but he didn't want them to give him any more trouble.   He sentenced Mo to work on a slave ship until he died.

From your point of view:

Was there anything fair about this court trial?

Was there anything unfair about this court trial?

3. A COURT IN ENGLAND IN THE MIDDLE AGES—1150 A.D.

A clergyman trained in law acted as judge in a certain town in England. A man named Mo was brought before him by the townspeople. They said that Mo had killed two people. The judge told Mo that God would decide his guilt or innocence. He said, "Mo, grab this red hot iron in your hand and hold it. Then your hand will be wrapped in cloth. After three days, the cloth will be removed. If your hand shows no sign of the scars of the burn, it will be a sign from God that you are innocent. If your hand shows signs of the burn, you will be found guilty and hanged by the neck until you die."

From your point of view:

Was there anything fair about this court trial?

Was there anything unfair about this court trial?

4. A MODERN COURT, 1950

Judge Clark had been appointed by the governor to be a judge in _____. Mo had been
(your state)
arrested by the police because they suspected him of killing two people. Mo was too poor to pay for a lawyer. The court appointed a lawyer for him. A jury of twelve people listened to the state prosecuting attorney present the case against Mo. Then they listened to Mo and his lawyer tell his side of the story. The court reporter was sick that day, so no record of what the witnesses said was kept. The jury decided that Mo had killed two people in a rage of anger. The judge took into consideration that Mo was in a rage of anger when he killed the two people. The judge gave Mo a prison sentence and said he could get out early for good behavior in prison.

From your point of view:

Was there anything fair about this court trial?

Was there anything unfair about this court trial?

1000 B.C.   1 B.C.   1034 A.D.   1980 A.D.

EXTRA!

At different times in history, people used different ways to resolve conflicts. Research some societies and periods in history to find out the methods people used to settle disputes. The librarian or your teacher could direct you to books on:

Ancient Egypt
Ancient Greece
Ancient Rome
Tribes in Africa
American Indians
Colonial America
Middle Ages in France

When reading these books, look for a specific society or period of history that interests you. Find information about government, laws, courts, or the legal system in that society.

Once you have found some information about how disputes were settled, you could draw pictures showing these procedures in a booklet. Or you could make up scenes and give mini-plays showing the methods used.

Note to teacher: Teachers have asked us to include some extra credit activities for students who are particularly interested in law-related education. Other teachers wanted to have some individualized research projects. We hope EXTRA EXTRA fulfills these needs.

DUE PROCESS IN THE COURTS

Objective: **Students will be able to define the term "due process of law."**

Students will interpret what certain constitutional rights mean in specific cases.

Due process means fair legal procedure. The Fifth and Fourteenth Amendments of the U.S. Constitution say "...nor [shall] any person be deprived of life, liberty, or property without due process of law." The amendments describe the rights of the people. For example, the

Amendment says, "In all criminal prosecutions, the accused shall enjoy the right to a speedy and public trial,...and to have the Assistance of Counsel for his defence."

It has been the job of judges in the United States to decide exactly what the right to "due process" means when people come to court. The case that follows is a true story about a man who said he did not receive due process of law (fair treatment) when he went to court because he didn't have a lawyer. In deciding his case, the judges had to interpret the right to "due process" and decide if it meant that an accused person should have a lawyer even if she/he is too poor to pay for one.

Pretend you are the judge.

How would you interpret what the Sixth Amendment means in the following case?

Note to teacher: You may want to take time here to make sure students know what the U.S. Constitution is. Lessons about the Constitution can be found in *Lawmaking*, Second Edition, Law in Action Series, West Publishing Company.

CASE I

THE GIDEON CASE
"RIGHT TO COUNSEL"

In 1961, Clarence Earl Gideon was found guilty and sent to jail in Florida for burglarizing a pool hall. While in prison, Gideon wrote the Supreme Court in Florida saying he did not get a fair trial because he did not have a lawyer. The Florida Supreme Court turned down his petition for a new trial. Then he wrote to the Supreme Court of the United States.

Note to teacher: *Gideon v. Wainwright,* 372 U.S. 335, 83 S.Ct. 792 (1963). The case is illustrated in a 23 minute film, *The Gideon Case, Justice Under the Law,* Our Living Bill of Rights Series from the Encyclopaedia Brittanica Educational Corporation.

The U.S. Supreme Court decided to hear and decide the issue raised by the Gideon case. Gideon argued that he did not get a fair trial because he was too poor to hire a lawyer. The opposing lawyer argued that Gideon did get a fair trial even without the help of a lawyer. He said that Gideon was of sound mind and able to defend himself. He said that courts could not supply a lawyer for every person who was too poor to hire one without additional cost to the taxpayer. The lawyer against Gideon argued that having the help of a lawyer was not essential to getting a fair trial.

QUESTIONS:

1. What is the case about?

2. What does the court have to decide?

3. If you were on the Court how would you decide Gideon's case? Give reasons for your answer.

4. Do you think having a lawyer defend you in court is necessary? Why?

5. Should the lawyers who defend people who are too poor to pay be expected to work without pay? Why?

6. What problems could arise if lawyers are required to volunteer their work instead of getting paid for it?

7. Where should the money come from to pay lawyers who defend poor people? Is it right for society to pay by using taxpayers' money?

8. If a lawyer is provided for poor people, should private investigators also be provided for people who cannot afford them? Why?

Note to teacher: The students will undoubtedly want to know the "right decision—the one the U.S. Supreme Court decided." There is no "right" answer, but only what the U.S. Supreme Court decided. In this case, the U.S. Supreme Court found that in criminal cases, where imprisonment is a possible sentence, the Sixth Amendment right to counsel imposes upon states, through the Fourteenth Amendment, an obligation to provide a lawyer for defendants who are too poor to hire a lawyer. According to the Court, this obligation exists because it is not possible to have a fair trial without the assistance of a lawyer. Laws and court procedures are so complex that a defendant with no legal training is not likely to be a fair match for a trained and experienced prosecutor. Have the class discuss the questions before telling them the decision made by the U.S. Supreme Court.

Try another case. The Sixth Amendment to the U.S. Constitution also says, "...in all criminal prosecutions (trials) the accused shall enjoy the right to a speedy and public trial...to be informed of the nature and the cause of the accusation, and to be confronted with the witnesses against him...."

Decide what these words mean in the following case.

CASE II

ILLINOIS v. ALLEN
"RIGHT TO CONFRONT WITNESSES"

In 1957, Allen had a trial and was convicted of armed robbery and sentenced to serve 10 to 30 years in prison. Later, Allen asked that his case be appealed (he filed a WRIT OF HABEAS CORPUS*) because he claimed he was not given his constitutional right to remain present during his trial and be confronted with witnesses against him. During his trial, Allen had yelled out at the judge and talked back to him.

*See Glossary, page 131, for definition.

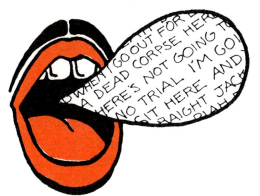

Allen: "When I go out for lunch you (judge) are going to be a corpse here."

Judge: "One more outbreak like that and I will remove you from the courtroom."

Allen: "There's not going to be no trial. I'm going to sit here and you're going to talk and you can bring your shackles out and straight jacket and put them on me, but it will do no good because there's not going to be no trial."

After a few more words, Allen was removed from the courtroom and the trial went on without him. Allen kept insisting that he be brought back into the courtroom. Each time he was brought in he started yelling.

Note to teacher: *Illinois v. Allen*, 397 U.S. 337 (1970). The U.S. Supreme Court found that the defendant lost his constitutional right to be present at his trial because 1) he had been warned that if he continued his disruptive behavior he would be removed from the courtroom, 2) his behavior was so disruptive and disrespectful that removal or restraint was justifiable, 3) charging him with criminal contempt would not have made him stop, and 4) he was informed that he could return to the courtroom if he agreed to act in an orderly manner.

WHAT DOES THE LAW MEAN IN THIS CASE?

INTERPRETATION

QUESTIONS:

1. Why do you think it is really important for an accused person to be present at his/her trial and see and hear the witnesses?

2. Should Allen be allowed to be present at his trial even though he was disrupting it? Please explain.

3. What are some of the other ways that the judge could have handled Allen?

4. Allen's outbursts showed he did not respect the order and dignity of a courtroom. Which value do you think is more important:

   a) That order and respect be kept in the courtroom at all times.

   b) That an accused person never be forced to give up his/her right to be present at the trial.

5. What if they gagged Allen and tied him up and sat him down in the courtroom? What problems would this solution create?

6. Should Allen have been put in a separate room with closed circuit T.V. so that he could see the trial if he wanted? What problems would this solution create?

Interpretation means the determination of what the words of the law mean. Whatever you decided in the Gideon and Allen cases, was an interpretation of the words of the Constitution. You were deciding what the Constitution means for today's world, in the same way that the Justices of the Supreme Court do.

PRECEDENT USED IN DECIDING CASES

Objective: Students will be able to explain how precedent is used in making court decisions.

It is the court's job to make decisions about the problems (or cases) that people bring before it. Judges write down their final decision and the reasons why they made that decision. When a similar problem arises, another judge can look up what was decided in the earlier case to help him/her make a decision. This earlier opinion is called a PRECEDENT. Judges try to keep their decisions consistent with precedents unless they have a very good reason not to. In a sense, courts make law when they make decisions which do not follow the rule of the precedent.

If you were a defendant in a criminal case and you wanted the court to appoint a lawyer for your defense what court case would you use as a precedent to support your argument?

Why is that case a precedent?

Note to teacher: see pages 25 and 26.

OTHER PEOPLE USE PRECEDENT IN MAKING DECISIONS, TOO.

Oliver was late for school with no excuse. Mr. Gibson, his teacher, decided that Oliver would have to stay after school to make up the time he missed.

Everyone knew that Mr. Gibson made Oliver stay after school.

A month later, Gene and Steve were late for school and had no excuse. Should Gene and Steve be made to stay after school too? Why?

When Mr. Gibson decided what to do with Oliver and told the class about it, he set a PRECEDENT in his classroom. After Oliver's case, all the other students should have realized the same rule about being late would probably apply to them.

Was it important (or fair) that Gene and Steve know they were going to be treated in the same way as Oliver? Why?

Should Mr. Gibson ever change his mind and treat a student who was late to school with no excuse differently? Why? Why not?

As society changes, new problems appear. What seemed like a good law once might not work well in the present. Judges try to make decisions which are consistent with decisions made before. If they believe that some law is not good for society anymore, they can

the precedent set earlier and change the law.

If the law changed every time a new case was decided, people would get confused about what is the law and what isn't. Judges need to keep up on what other judges' opinions have been, so that they can apply the law consistently.

Now try to figure out which precedent applies to the four cases on the next three pages. Each of the answers, A, B, and C is a real decision by a court but only one of them applies to each case.

Note to teacher: The following cases are difficult reading. The cases are given in their order of difficulty. Students in a wide range of classrooms have found that they were challenged and stimulated by the format. This lesson teaches critical thinking skills and reinforces necessary reading skills. However, because of the difficulty, some teachers have read the cases to the students. To involve the entire class, rather than have one student giving the answer, you might try this suggestion. Ask the students to hold up a number of fingers to indicate their answer to each of the four cases. If the answer is A when you count to three they would hold up the forefinger. If the answer is B two fingers and C they would hold up three fingers.

1 A man building a bookcase misses the nail and smashes his finger with a hammer. He sues the hardware store where he bought the hammer. He wants the store to pay for his medical expenses and his pain. The hardware store claims it should not have to pay the man.

Which of the following statements by a court is a *precedent* for this case?

A. A store does not have to pay for injuries which result from using a tool for a purpose which is different from what people usually use it for.

B. A store must pay for injuries which result from a person using a tool in the usual way if the store does not tell the person about the danger of using it.

C. A store does not pay for injuries which result from a person using a tool in the usual way and the danger of using the tool is obvious to anyone.

Note to teacher: C is correct precedent

2 Benjie Purdue, a tenant at Happy Forest Apartments, complained to the city housing inspector about the condition of his apartment. The inspector came out and looked the whole building over. She gave the owner, Mr. Olsen, a ticket for having dangerous conditions at the apartment building. Mr. Olsen got mad and told Benjie he had to move out. Benjie didn't move because he liked living in the apartment. The owner sued Benjie to make him move out.

Which of the following statements of law is a *precedent* for this case?

A. A landlord does not have to have a good reason when he tells a tenant to move, but he cannot do it for a reason like retaliation. (Retaliation means getting back at someone for making a complaint to the government.)

B. A landlord can tell a tenant to move out if the tenant breaks a rule of the apartment building.

C. A landlord can tell a tenant to move if someone in the landlord's family wants to live in the apartment.

Note to teacher: A is correct precedent

3 Marcie Coleman's son Todd, 12 years old, has to stay in bed all the time because of a bad back problem. Todd could have an operation on his back which might make him able to sit and maybe even to stand. Mrs. Coleman will not allow the operation to be performed because she has a religious belief that all health problems can be solved by God's will without surgery or medicine. A social worker asks the juvenile court to find that Todd is a "neglected child" because of his mother's refusal to provide him necessary medical treatment. The social worker also asks the court to order the operation to be performed. Mrs. Coleman claims that the First Amendment to the Constitution gives her freedom of religion.

Which of the following statements by a court is a *precedent* for this case?

A. Freedom of religion includes the freedom to refuse a certain medical treatment because of religious beliefs about treatment, except where the treatment is necessary to protect the rest of community from a disease.

B. Freedom of religion includes the freedom of a parent to refuse medical treatment for a minor child because of religious beliefs about treatment, except where the treatment is necessary to save the minor's life or to treat a serious medical condition.

C. Freedom of religion does not include freedom to give a minor drugs for religious purposes where use of the drugs is dangerous to the minor's health.

Note to teacher: B is correct precedent

4 Martin Still was arrested for driving under the influence of drugs. At the police station, the police force Martin to let a doctor take blood from Martin's finger so the police could show there was evidence of drugs in his body. When the government tried to use the blood sample at Martin's trial, Martin claimed that it was unfair to use his blood as evidence because the Fifth Amendment of the Constitution gives him the right against self-incrimination (the right not to be forced to testify against oneself).

Which of the following statements by a court is a *precedent* in this case?

A. The right against self-incrimination applies to a confession a suspect makes after being beaten up. The government cannot use the confession as evidence because the person was forced to testify against himself/herself.

B. The right against self-incrimination does not apply to blood found on the suspect's coat. The government can use this blood as evidence because the suspect does not testify against himself.

C. The right against self-incrimination does not apply to finger-prints, photographs, and other evidence taken of the body of a suspect. The government can use fingerprints, photographs, and other evidence of the body because the suspect does not testify against himself/herself.

Note to teacher: C is correct precedent. However, in determining whether the evidence can actually be used, other factors may be applicable. For instance, evidence taken before police had advised the suspect of his/her constitutional rights may be excluded on the basis of the "exclusionary rule" which prevents the use in a criminal trial of illegally seized evidence.

Choosing which statement by a court is a PRECEDENT for a case can be difficult. But, the real difficulty for the courts comes from the fact that often there may be precedents favorable to each side of a conflict. The judges must decide which precedent is better in terms of the reasoning in the decisions, the values, and the effects of applying each decision.

Each case on the next two pages is followed by two precedents. Which precedent would you follow in deciding the case? In making your decision think about: the reasons that support each precedent, the values involved (what is important to people?), the effect this precedent would have on people's lives.

Divide the class into groups with uneven numbers of members (3, 5, 7). Read case 1, about the entertainer's monkey. Discuss which precedent you think should be used, giving the reasons for your choice. The precedent chosen by the majority of students in the group is the "majority opinion." The precedent chosen by the rest of the group is the "minority opinion." In each group a spokesperson for the "majority opinion" and one for the "minority opinion" should be prepared to present the opinion and reasons for the opinion to the class.

Do case 2, about the performer at the state fair, in the same way.

Note to teacher: You may want to have the class vote on the precedents. Case 1 is a compilation of cases; case 2 is based entirely on an actual United States Supreme Court case.

1 Jimmy is an entertainer. Part of his act involves dancing with a monkey known as "Mork the Monk". Jimmy has had Mork for six years and they have become good "pals" even when they are not performing. Mork wears clothes, sits in a high chair at meals and goes everywhere with Jimmy on his motorcycle. All of Jimmy's friends love Mork and treat him just like he is a regular member of the group. One day Mork bites a stranger who comes to the house. The stranger sues Jimmy and says Jimmy must pay his medical bills. Jimmy claims Mork has never hurt anyone before.

Both of the following statements about law are precedents for this case. Which one would you apply? Why?

A. A person who owns an animal which the law considers to be "wild" must pay for all injuries the animal causes whether or not the person knew the animal might injure someone. "Wild" animals are animals which are naturally ferocious and not tameable, such as lions, tigers, bears, wolves, and elephants.

B. A person who owns an animal which the law considers to be "tame" must pay for injuries the animal causes only if the person knows that the animal has a mean streak or that the animal is likely to injure someone. "Tame" animals are animals which are tameable and may be used by people for work or food or as house pets, such as dogs and cats, sheep, and cattle.

2 One of the performers at a state fair has a special act. He gets shot out of a cannon like a cannonball! The act lasts only 2 minutes. A television news program shows his whole act on the news without his permission. The performer sues the news station for using his act without paying him. The news station claims that the Constitution guarantees freedom of the press.

Which of the following precedents would you follow? Why?

A. The news media (newspapers, magazines, TV, radio, etc.) may report on a person who is in the public view even if the person doesn't want to be in the news. However, the news media may not report information about a person with the purpose of injuring him/her.

B. A performer has the right to control the use of his/her act; no one else may use his/her act for their own benefit even if they do not make money from using it.

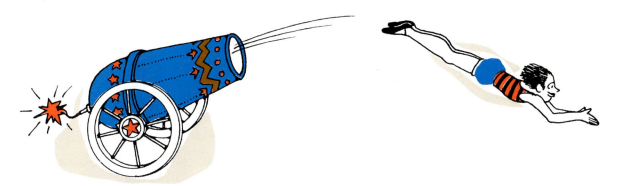

Note to student: The U.S. Supreme Court decided this case after one of the parties APPEALED the case. The party believed the judgment of the state supreme court of Ohio was not fair, and appealed to the U.S. Supreme Court. The next lesson will help you learn more about appeals.

Note to teacher: This is a real case, *Zacchine v. Scripps-Howard Broadcasting,* 433 U.S. 562 (1977), in which the U.S. Supreme Court found for the performer. The Constitution "does not immunize media when they broadcast a performer's entire act without his consent." The Court said that the fact that the performance was shown on the news was irrelevant to whether the station should pay; in essence, it was the same as showing a play or movie on TV without paying the royalties.

APPEALING YOUR CASE

Objective: **Students will be able to explain the difference between a trial court and an appeals court.**

Students will participate in a mock appeals court case.

WHY HAVE COURTS OF APPEAL?

This story might help you answer this question:

Pretend that

are watching a baseball game and your favorite team has two outs and one player on third. It is the last inning of the game. If they win this game, they go to the World Series. The batter hits a grounder. The pitcher gets the ball and throws it to home plate. You are sure the runner made it, but the umpire says "OUT".

When the instant replay is shown on TV everyone could see the umpire was wrong.

Judges can make mistakes when they decide cases. Sometimes the mistakes made by trial court judges are not their fault. An example would be when a trial court judge fails to give a defendant a certain right before the Supreme Court has interpreted the Constitution to require that right. Giving people the right to appeal their case to another court is the way the court system tries to deal with mistakes judges make in interpreting the law or in trial procedure.

What is the difference between a trial court and a court of appeals?

TRIAL COURT

Has one judge and usually a jury.

Hears evidence.

Hears witnesses.

Judge or jury makes a decision about the outcome of the case.

APPEALS COURT

Has several judges but no juries.

Hears arguments of lawyers.

Lawyers send written copies of their arguments to the judges before the lawyers personally appear in court.

Reviews whether the law in the trial court was applied correctly or whether the evidence correctly supported the decision.

If the judges agree with the trial court, they affirm its decision. If they disagree, they reverse or overrule the trial judge.

But they cannot say that a person who was found guilty by a trial court is really not guilty. They can say that some part of that person's trial was unfair and the trial court judge should hold another trial for him/her.

In a court of appeals:

An appeal can not be made by the prosecution, only by the defendant in a criminal case.

An appeal to the U.S. Supreme Court can be made only on a constitutional issue. For example: if your client was found guilty in a state criminal court, you can appeal to the state supreme court. Your state supreme court is the highest court to which you can appeal unless your client has not been given his/her constitutional rights. But if your client's constitutional rights have been denied, you can take the case all the way to the U.S. Supreme Court. You would be studying law books to find all the precedents and the laws of your state that apply to this case.

TAKE THIS CASE FROM THE [COURT OF APPEALS] TO THE [SUPREME COURT]

The case: Defendant Laney Howard, age 26, was accused of holding up a small grocery store. The grocery clerk identified Laney as the man who came into the store and ordered him to open the cash register. The clerk said he thought he saw a gun in Laney's pocket. Someone saw Laney and the clerk through the store window and called the police. The police arrested Laney as he was running from the store. The police found only a water pistol in Laney's pocket. Laney's case came to trial in the criminal trial division of the circuit court. The grocery clerk said he was afraid because he believed Laney had a gun in his pocket. Laney was accused of armed robbery and carrying a concealed weapon.

The trial court found Laney guilty of the charges. The judge decided that in this case the water pistol should be considered a concealed weapon, and so the crime was armed robbery.

The law says:

Armed robbery is taking property from a person by force or threat of force by:

(1) being armed with a deadly weapon.

(2) using or threatening to use a deadly weapon.

A deadly weapon is anything made or used in a way to lead a reasonable person to believe it deadly or dangerous.

Carrying a concealed weapon means carrying a hidden weapon or other things designed to kill or cause great bodily harm.

Note to teacher: This definition is taken from Arizona law.

The Appeal:

Laney's lawyer appealed the case saying that a water pistol is not a weapon in this case and therefore Laney could not be found guilty of armed robbery or carrying a concealed weapon.

The appeals court affirmed the trial court's decision and Laney's lawyer appealed to the state supreme court.

DO YOU THINK THAT THE WATER PISTOL SHOULD BE CONSIDERED A WEAPON IN THIS CASE?

One-half of class decides to argue yes—the water pistol should be considered a weapon in this case.

One-half of class decides to argue no—the water pistol should not be considered a weapon in this case.

1. Begin by working with a partner to develop good reasons for supporting your side of this case on appeal.

2. Then get together in your Yes or No group. In the group, go over everyone's reasons.

What were the best arguments on the "Yes side"? Discuss with one another what you think the best arguments were. These arguments should be written down and submitted as "briefs" to the judges on the supreme court.

What were the best arguments on the "No side"? Discuss with one another what you think the best arguments were. These arguments should be written down and submitted as "briefs" to the judges on the supreme court.

1. The judges should read the briefs carefully. While they are doing that in a corner of the room (their court chambers), each side should select one or two people and help them to present the oral argument for that side.

2. The judges on the supreme court will listen to both sides of the argument and make a decision. They must explain the reasons for their decisions. They all do not have to agree. The decision that most of the judges agree with is called the *majority opinion*. If any judge disagrees with this opinion, his or her opinion is called the *dissenting opinion*.

3. The majority opinion becomes the law; it sets a precedent that courts will follow in future cases like this.

Many courts give out information pamphlets which explain the court proceedings. By asking your local courts, or the local or state bar association (an association for attorneys), you should be able to obtain copies of these pamphlets. These pamphlets are the only way some people learn what to expect when they go to court. But sometimes these pamphlets are not helpful because they are so hard to read and difficult to understand. Read and study the pamphlets in class. Pick out important facts from them. Think of ways to design your own pamphlets. Make them easy to read and appealing to look at. They must be factual. Give your "student-designed" pamphlets to the local bar association or to the chief clerk at the courthouse.

Objective: **Students will be able to define a list of words introduced in Section I.**

Pick out any of these words that you are pretty sure you already know and write their meaning. Ask a classmate to check your work. Write the definition from the glossary of any words you miss or that you don't know, using the glossary on pages 127 to 131.

conflict ⎯⎯⎯⎯⎯⎯⎯⎯⎯⎯⎯⎯⎯⎯

resolve ⎯⎯⎯⎯⎯⎯⎯⎯⎯⎯⎯⎯⎯⎯

civil case ⎯⎯⎯⎯⎯⎯⎯⎯⎯⎯⎯⎯

criminal case ⎯⎯⎯⎯⎯⎯⎯⎯⎯⎯

jurisdiction ⎯⎯⎯⎯⎯⎯⎯⎯⎯⎯⎯

procedure ⎯⎯⎯⎯⎯⎯⎯⎯⎯⎯⎯

due process of law ⎯⎯⎯⎯⎯⎯⎯

precedent ⎯⎯⎯⎯⎯⎯⎯⎯⎯⎯⎯

appeal ⎯⎯⎯⎯⎯⎯⎯⎯⎯⎯⎯⎯⎯

interpret ⎯⎯⎯⎯⎯⎯⎯⎯⎯⎯⎯⎯

Make up sentences that leave one word to be filled in by a classmate. Like this:

1. In deciding the case the judge had to look up the ⎯⎯precedent⎯⎯ to see what other judges decided.
2. When a court has power to settle certain kinds of conflicts it has ⎯⎯jurisdiction⎯⎯ in that area.

NEWSBULLETIN REVIEW—SECTION I

Objective: **Students will be able to answer questions on a class test about information presented in Section I.**

Note to students: This lesson is a review quiz. You can use it to check how much you have learned so far about courts and trials. Some classes have turned these reviews into newsbulletins. When your answers get printed in a newsbulletin, they help other people learn what you have learned.

The next pages give you an idea of what the finished newsbulletin might look like. It was done by another class. Take a look . . .

Note to teacher: Have the students turn to the blank newsbulletin on page 47. The class may vote on the name or letterhead of the newsbulletin. Then, each student should complete every section of the newsbulletin by answering the questions or giving his/her opinion.

The newsbulletin technique can be used as the evaluation measure or test. The "best" articles can be printed on ditto masters and made to look like a real newspaper. The newsbulletin should stimulate the students to try hard to answer all the questions on the "test."

THE COOK COURT REPORTER

Name	Edition	School

Editorial

After studying the first part of **Courts and Trials,** what do you think is the most important thing that you have learned????   Why??

I think more people should understand how our court system works so that they will appreciate the good things and work to change things that are not very good like the bail system and the time cases take to come to trial.

Stephen

People should see that there are other ways of handling conflicts besides fighting and that there are many different kinds of courts.   On T.V. there seems to be only one kind of court, but we have learned that there are different kinds of courts for different kinds of problems.

Reginald

Crossword Puzzle

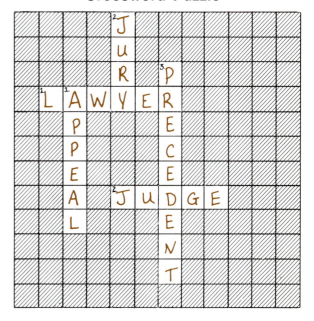

Across

1. A person who has been licensed to represent others in legal matters.
2. A person appointed or elected to hear cases and decide questions of law.

Down

1. Take a case to a higher court for review.
2. A group of people chosen by law, and satisfactory to both sides, to decide the facts of a case.
3. Courts follow _____ when they use previous court decisions for guidance in deciding questions of law in a similar case.

Students who had correct answers to crossword puzzles were Andrea, Cindy, Stephen, Robert, and Sam.

Art Editorial

Make a collage of different ways of handling conflicts using your own drawings, or cut out pictures from magazines. Circle the way you think is best and give your reasons why.

There are all kinds of major conflicts. My picture shows the Congress of Vienna solving a big conflict between countries (World War I). But for many other kinds of conflicts a jury trial is the best way to handle the conflict because people can say their reasons, have witnesses and then the jury decides.

Susan

Are these statements TRUE or FALSE?

1. The Judge always decides if an accused person is guilty or not.

    False

2. The Court does have power to have people pay fines and to imprison them.

    True

3. An example of a civil case would be if two people went to court because there was a breach of contract.

    True

Students who had correct answers were Robert, Susan, Alice, Cindy, Brea, Terry, Heide, Damon, Clairice, Allen, Stephen.

NEWSBULLETIN

RESOLVING CONFLICTS

Explain what you think is the best way to resolve this conflict. Give well-thought-out reasons to support your decision.

CARTOON

Draw a picture of a person doing something and describe the conflict that might arise as a result of the action.

TRUE/FALSE

1. Federal courts handle cases involving the U.S. Constitution.
   True

2. The series of steps courts follow in deciding cases is called legal procedure.   True

3. Judges do not consider decisions made by other judges when deciding a case.   False

4. If a judge or a lawyer makes a mistake during a trial there is nothing a defendant can do.   False

5. U.S. Supreme Court justices have decided that people accused of serious crimes have a right to have a lawyer at their trial even if they are too poor to pay for one.   True

WHICH COURT WOULD YOU GO TO?

1. If you wanted to get a divorce, your case would be handled in _____.   domestic relations court

2. If a fifteen-year-old was taken into custody for shoplifting, the case would be handled in _____.   juvenile court

Note to teacher: The purpose of the second section of lessons is to help students understand the judicial process by learning about the roles of people involved in the courts and how their roles affect legal procedure. Pilot teachers have used these lessons as an opportunity to have students learn about careers in law as well. For students who are interested in pursuing information about legal careers, we have included an EXTRA EXTRA assignment on pages 72 and 73.

SECTION II
LAWYERS AS CONFLICT RESOLVERS

LESSON 11

Objective: **Students will be able to explain the role of lawyers as negotiators.**

Students will be able to practice negotiating a case.

Lawyers help people resolve problems when they can't do it by themselves. A lawyer is a person who acts for other people in dealing with their legal problems.

One way that lawyers attempt to resolve conflicts is to negotiate— discuss the problem and try to reach a **RESOLUTION** through compromise rather than in the courts. Compromise means giving up part of what you want in order to get something from the other side.

For example:

"We want at least $6,000 in damages to repay Mr. Green for the injuries he received in the accident."

"The facts show that the accident was partly Mr. Green's fault, therefore my client, Mrs. Braken, should not have to pay Mr. Green for all damages he suffered. Instead of $6,000 we will agree to pay him $1,000."

If the two parties cannot reach a compromise on what is an acceptable solution outside of court, then they may decide to take their case to court and have a jury or a judge decide.

When a lawyer negotiates, he or she does not decide who was right and who was wrong in the case. The lawyers listen to both sides and try to come up with an agreement that both sides will accept.

Lawyers may act as negotiators in cases involving crimes. The defendant's lawyer might "plea bargain" with the prosecutor, "My client will plead guilty if you ask the judge to reduce the sentence." If the lawyers, defendant, and the judge agree on the "bargain" the case will be settled and not go to trial.

When a lawyer takes a case he/she assumes the responsibility to argue in favor of his/her client to win the case or obtain the most favorable settlement.

Now you will negotiate for your client and try to reach a compromise without going to court.

Divide into groups of three. In Story 1, one person will be the lawyer representing Molly's family, one person will be the lawyer representing Frances' family, and one person will be the observer. In Story 2, one person will represent Matt, one person will represent Frank, and one person will be the observer. Decide which of the stories you want to work on. The two lawyers should discuss the case and try to reach an agreement acceptable to their clients. The observer should listen carefully because at the end of the negotiations, the observer will report to the class. He/she should explain what happened in the "negotiation." Was an agreement reached? If so, what was it? If not, what were the problems?

Story 1 Molly and Frances

Frances and Molly walked down the hall in between classes. They were jokingly pushing and shoving each other saying "got you last." When Frances bent over to drink from the water fountain Molly gave her one last push. Frances hit the water spout hard. She cut her lip and chipped three of her front teeth. The dentist bill was $600. Frances will have capped teeth for the rest of her life. Frances' family believes Molly or her family should pay the dentist bill. Molly's family believes Frances brought the injury on herself and that Frances' family should pay all of the dentist bill.

Story 2 Frank and Matt

Frank, 22, sold Matt, 21, his five year old Chevy. They wrote out a contract which said, "I Matt Hughes, agree to buy Frank Olsen's Chevy for $1500 to be paid in monthly payments of $100 for 15 months. They both signed and dated the contract and had a neighbor witness the contract. Frank needed the $100 a month from Matt to pay for the new car he bought for himself. After two months, Matt told Frank that the car kept breaking down. Matt said that he would not pay Frank any more money. He wanted to return the car, cancel the contract and get back the money he already paid. Frank said, "a deal was a deal." Frank said Matt owed him the remaining $1300.

LAWYERS AND ASKING QUESTIONS

Objective: **Students will be able to recognize effective questioning techniques.**

Students will analyze their questions to determine if they effectively bring out the facts.

When lawyers are unable to reach a compromise, the person with the complaint may decide to take the case to court or trial. A trial is a formal proceeding in court in which the solution is reached by a judge or a jury.

In a trial, lawyers act as adversaries. They represent opposing sides in the case. Our system of justice is based on the idea that when the lawyers on opposing sides of a case present their arguments based on the facts, the jury or the judge will be able to determine the truth of what happened and make a fair, or "just" decision.

"I will prove that the car accident in which Mr. Green was injured happened because of Mrs. Braken's carelessness. Mrs. Braken should pay Mr. Green $6,000."

"I will prove that the accident was not entirely Mrs. Braken's fault. Mrs. Braken should not have to pay Mr. Green anything."

Note to student: Most lawyers do not spend much time in court. Some never appear in a courtroom. Lawyers handle different areas of the law. They may deal in juvenile, tax, family, or environmental law and may spend most of their time doing research in their special area of interest.

Lawyers need special training to do their work. After four years of college, most lawyers spend three years in law school. They learn about the law, how to research laws which apply to a particular case. In addition, they develop skills in negotiating and asking questions.

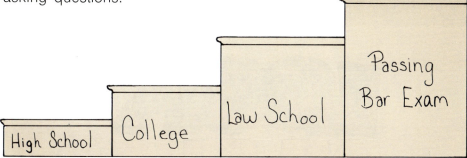

Trial Lawyers should be able to

1. Research the law and decide whether it fits the particular case.
2. State convincingly their side of the case and support their arguments with reasons and evidence.
3. Ask questions to get out the facts of the case.

Lawyers must know how to ask good questions that bring out the facts of the case. Before a trial, lawyers spend time preparing questions they will ask each witness.

The following statements are from two students who took part in a mock trial at their school.

"I played the prosecuting attorney in our criminal mock trial. (Attorney is another word for lawyer.) As prosecuting attorney, I work for the state. We did the case in Lesson 24. I was supposed to try to prove the defendant guilty. I didn't realize how much time I would have to spend preparing the case. On T.V., the lawyer never seems to spend time preparing. But there, someone writes a script. Real trials aren't like that. Asking the right questions is very important."

"I played the defense lawyer in our trial. I tried to prove the defendant was not guilty. I didn't realize that writing good questions would take so much preparation time. It made me think about the information I wanted to get through the questions."

In order to do a good job for a client, a lawyer must know all the facts of the case. The lawyer investigates: What happened? To whom did it happen? Why did it happen? The lawyer asks questions to get as much information as possible about the case.

In order to help Mrs. Smith in the case below, a lawyer would need to:

WHO · WHAT · WHERE · WHEN · HOW

WHO · WHAT · WHERE · WHEN · HOW

Mrs. Smith was driving south on Kingshighway. She says she stopped for a red light. When the light turned green she moved forward. Her car was struck on the right side by a car driven by Mr. Atwater.

To investigate the case what questions would you ask your client, Mrs. Smith. Put your questions on the board. Which questions are most helpful? Why are some questions better than others?

The lawyers look over all the information they have gathered through the investigation and develop their questions for trial—questions that will bring out only the information that is best for their client. In a trial, the lawyers, as adversaries, try to prove their side by asking witnesses questions which will bring out the information they want.

You will be given the opportunity to play a trial lawyer. As an adversary, present your side of the case by asking questions

In law school you would learn rules of questioning.

(1) Questions must be relevant. They must have something to do with the case. A lawyer from the other side can object that a question is IRRELEVANT (has nothing to do with the case). Then the judge must say whether the question can be asked.

(2) On DIRECT examination (this is when the lawyer questions the witness from his or her side) the lawyer can't ask LEADING questions. For example, "Isn't it true that you were in Chicago the night of the crime?" is a leading question, because it calls for the answer "yes." The question should be stated as: "Were you in Chicago on the night of the crime?" or "Where were you on the night of the crime?"

(3) On CROSS-EXAMINATION the opposing side asks the witness questions which attempt to call into doubt the truth or accuracy of what the witness said on direct examination.

Read this fact situation carefully:

Bob Smith, an 18-year-old student at Southeast High School, was accused of stealing an eight track tape player. The tape player was stolen from an automobile owned by Tim Jones, who lived at 4927 Grand. Jones reported that his tape player was stolen at 9 p.m., March 4, 1980. He said someone had broken into his car, a black Ford, and had taken the tape player. At 9:15, Barbara Thompson, who lived at 4929 Grand, reported to the police that she had seen a young man breaking into a car in front of her home at about 9 p.m. She said she thought the young man was Bob Smith, who lived one house west. The police found Bob Smith at his home at 10:30 p.m. Bob told them that he was at a friend's house from 5 p.m. to 10 p.m. that night. The police took Smith to the station. The tape player was never found.

Ask half the class members to pretend they are the prosecutors, the lawyers who will try to prove that Bob Smith is guilty of the charge against him. You want to get your side of the case presented effectively.

Who would you call into court as witnesses?

Make a *List* of the important questions you would ask each witness.

Are any of the questions leading?

Did you ask any irrelevant questions?

Go back over your questions. Correct any that aren't effective.

Ask half the class members to pretend they are the defense lawyers, the lawyers who will try to prove that Bob Smith was not guilty of the charge. You want to get your side of the case presented effectively.

Who would you call into court as witnesses?

Make a *List* of the important questions you would ask each witness.

Are any of the questions leading?

Did you ask any irrelevant questions?

Go back over your questions. Correct any that aren't effective.

Note to student: Remember that according to the Fifth Amendment, Bob Smith, the defendant, does not have to testify against himself. The defense lawyer, with permission from Bob Smith, can call him as a witness. The prosecution cannot call Bob Smith. But once he is called as a witness, the prosecution can cross-examine him.

Note to teacher: Students might work in groups of 3 or 4 to work out the questions they will ask the witnesses.

To expand this activity students could be chosen to play the witnesses. Representatives from each side could be the prosecuting attorney and the defense attorney. The class could enact a mini-mock trial where the lawyers from both sides take turns asking the witnesses the questions. Students should save the best questions from this activity, as they will be needed for page 59.

EVIDENCE

Objective: **Students will be able to explain what kind and how much evidence is necessary to decide a case.**

Students will recognize different kinds of evidence.

Divide class into two groups. Read the story* and then decide what would be the fair thing to do:

Mrs. Jordan said that she would pay George, Pete, and Allen $10.00 a week if they would take care of her yard. She said that if they would come every week without fail, she would give each of them a special Christmas present, too. Allen missed a week. When Christmas came, George and Pete got special presents, but Allen did not. Do you think it was fair that Allen did not get a present? Why? Why not?

Discuss this question with your own group. Then discuss your decision and your reasons for it with the other group.

Note to teacher: An additional fact—Tell one of the groups (without the other group hearing) that Allen's mother had to go to the hospital and that Allen had to stay home to take care of his younger sister. One story will then have different facts. When the two groups discuss their decisions, they should discover the difference. Then ask the students if the additional FACT about Allen's mother being in the hospital made one group think differently about the story. Sometimes students decide that the one fact does not make any difference. Why is it important to have all the facts? (Even if that fact wouldn't make any difference in the *way* the group thought about the case.) An important point to note is who decides when a fact is vital to the case.

Emphasize that all the FACTS having to do with the story must be brought out before someone can make a good decision about what should be done.

*idea for story taken from Susan Davison Archer, elementary law-related education specialist.

Write down what you think is happening in this picture. Who are these people? What are they doing? Make up your own explanation of this picture without discussing it with anyone.

When everyone is finished, discuss everyone's explanation of this picture. Did people disagree about what is happening? Why do you think people see things in different ways?

It is hard to find out the correct facts in a situation because people see the same thing in different ways. Courts depend on FACTUAL INFORMATION (facts that prove what happened) when deciding a case.

Juries and judges must listen to the facts of the case. Lawyers present all the facts they can to make their argument believable to the jury or judge deciding the case.

When these facts are brought out in court, they are called

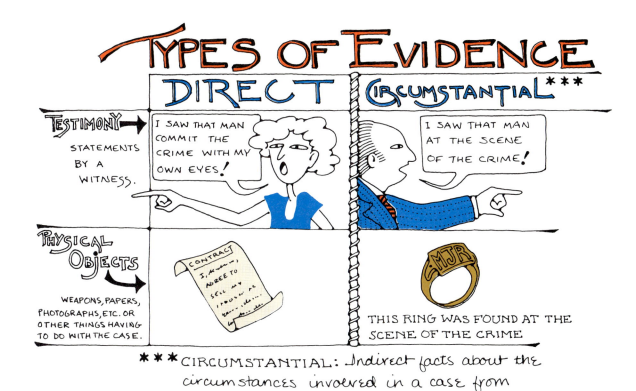

*** CIRCUMSTANTIAL: *Indirect facts about the circumstances involved in a case from which you can figure out how the event might have happened.*

Sometimes certain evidence cannot be considered by the judge or jury because it cannot be trusted to be true. Some examples of evidence which may be kept out of the trial are:

1. Hearsay evidence—second-hand evidence; something the witness did not see or hear personally. For example: "I heard my friend tell Bob that she really wanted an eight-track tape player." This statement would not be allowed in court.

2. Any evidence—objects or even words—which the police obtained in violation of the accused person's rights. There are rules police must follow when getting evidence. If police ignore these rules, the lawyer for the accused person can object to having the evidence presented.

It is up to each lawyer to object to (ask the judge not to allow) evidence which may not be trustworthy, or which was wrongly obtained.

Reread the list of questions you wrote for the previous lesson. What type of evidence were you asking for? Direct? Circumstantial? Physical? Did you ask for any evidence which may not be trustworthy?

JUDGE'S RESPONSIBILITIES

LeSSON 14

Objective: **Students will be able to explain two of the responsibilities a judge has during a trial.**

Students will participate in a sentencing procedure.

A judge has the power and legal authority to make decisions about what happens in his or her courtroom. With this authority, a judge also has the responsibility to make sure legal procedures are followed during a trial.

The following questions were asked of judges by students in different parts of the country.

From Austin, Texas

"How did you get to be a judge?"

"I was elected by voters of my city. As a circuit judge I must stand election every two years."

"As a juvenile judge, I must be voted on by the people in the metropolitan area where I live every two years."

"I was appointed by the Governor to be on the State Supreme Court."

From Sandy, Utah

"What is your biggest responsibility as a judge?"

"I would say deciding a sentence within the boundaries of the law."

"Always trying to be fair to everyone in the trial. I am a person too. I must decide objections based on the law and not on personal feelings."

You might want to interview a judge in your area. What kinds of questions would you ask? For more information read the community involvement project on page 66.

Note to teacher: How judges get to be judges varies from state to state. If you and your students interview a judge you could ask what the policies are in your area.

During a trial the judge acts like a referee making sure that rules of law are followed. Part of this responsibility includes handling objections made during a trial.

A judge must decide what to do if one of the lawyers objects to something said or done in the trial. To make good decisions about objections, a judge should know beforehand the facts of the case, the laws concerning such facts, and the laws about the kinds of questions that can be asked during a trial. Lawyers should not ask questions that

—don't have anything to do with the case (irrelevant)

—browbeat the witness

—lead the witness to give the answer the lawyer wants (leading questions)

—ask the witness to give hearsay evidence or to present evidence that was obtained in violation of the defendant's constitutional rights.

you were the judge in the case of *Floyd Walker v. Peggy Miller*?

Floyd's lawyer says, "Were you having problems with your marriage at the time of the car accident?"

Peggy's lawyer says, "I object, your Honor. I don't believe that has anything to do with whether she is to blame for the accident."

Think about how you would rule if you were the judge.

If you **OVERRULE** the objection—the lawyer can ask the question and the witness must answer.

If you **SUSTAIN** the objection—the witness does not have to answer and the lawyer must not ask the question again.

Before you decide think about these questions:

—Do you think Peggy's personal problems have anything to do with the accident?

—Are there any reasons for not allowing the lawyer to ask that question?

—What else must you know before making a decision?

How would you decide? _____ Overrule or _____ Sustain (check your decision)

Why? _____

_____

_____

Sentencing is another important responsibility of a judge. In criminal trials the judge must sentence (decide the punishment for) a defendant who has been found guilty or who has pleaded guilty. In a jury trial, the jury, rather than the judge, decides if the defendant is guilty or innocent. However, a defendant can waive (choose not to have) a jury trial. In that case, the judge decides the guilt or innocence of the defendant based on the facts of the case and also sentences the defendant if he/she is found guilty. In deciding the sentence, the judge considers the seriousness of the crime that was committed, the background of the defendant, and his/her present situation. There are certain standards judges must follow in deciding sentences.

The next pages in this lesson ask you to take on one of the responsibilities of a judge.

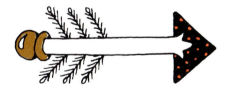

Before deciding upon a sentence, the judge reads a pre-sentence report giving information about the defendant. This information is obtained through interviews with the defendant, his/her relatives and friends, and anyone else who can give information about the defendant's background.

Presentence reports give information about:	Sample questions:
the offense	What crime are you accused of?
the defendant's version of the offense	Did you do it? If so, why did you do it?
any prior record	Have you had any trouble with the law before?
education of defendant	How many years of education did you have?
family history of defendant	Tell us something about your family. Are you married? Any children? Do you have brothers and sisters? Do you have responsibilities at home?
military service	Have you served in the Armed Forces? What kind of discharge do you have?
financial condition of defendant	Do you have a job? Do you own a home? Do you rent an apartment?
	(Think up some of your own questions)

These four people have been found guilty of various crimes.

1. Ruth Cook:

   47 years old, businesswoman; found guilty of evading taxes and writing bad checks amounting to $25,000.

   Standards:

   Evading taxes: Imprisonment up to 6 months, or fine not to exceed $500 or both.

   Bad checks: Imprisonment, between 0 and 10 years.

2. James White:

   18 years old, poor educational background; found guilty of burglary (stealing $2,500 worth of goods)

   Standards:

   Burglary: Imprisonment for not less than one year and not more than ten years.

3. Edna Marsha Lee:

   25 years old, mother of two small children, divorced; found guilty of shoplifting $200 worth of merchandise.

   Standards:

   If found guilty of grand theft, probably imprisonment for 1 to 10 years.

   If found guilty of misdemeanor theft probably imprisonment of up to 90 days and/or a fine of $300 to $500.

4. John Gates:

   32 years old, shoe salesman, father of three children; found guilty of manslaughter—killing a woman while driving when drunk.

   Standards:

   Manslaughter: Imprisonment for 5 to 10 years.

Divide into groups. Each group take one of the cases. One person in the group pretend to be the defendant. The other members of the group ask the "defendant" questions to gather information for a presentence report. Model your questions after the questions in the sample presentence form.

Each group should make up a presentence report from the answers given by the "defendant".

Based on the presentence report and the facts given above, recommend a SENTENCE that you think is fair for the "defendant" you interviewed. Explain the reasons for your sentence as the class discusses them.

Note to teacher: Have each group discuss the sentence it chooses. Students could compare their reasons for deciding on a particular sentence.

It is often difficult to have a judge come to your school. Judges are usually in court during school hours. If you have a field trip to the courthouse you might be able to interview a judge. (Arrangements for this would have to be made beforehand). If this is not possible, you might consider asking your questions in a letter to a judge.

Classes have done this in several different ways. You can get the names of judges in the various courts in your town from a courthouse information office or from the local bar association. The class could divide into groups and each group could write to a specific judge. Or, as a class you might write to a judge.

You could think about the questions you want to ask. Perhaps it would help to put all of the questions on the chalkboard and then decide which you really want answered. It is important to remember that judges are busy; six or seven questions are probably all he/she would have time to answer. You should show your understanding of the demands on the judges' time by thinking about the questions and asking only the most useful ones.

One class used the reply it received from the judge about jobs in the courts as part of a newsletter which it produced for other students and parents. Some classes made bulletin boards based on the letters they received.

Note to teacher: Sometimes the local bar association has available a resume of the judges' experience and training. Several classes have written to judges who were alumni of their elementary school. This project serves to focus discussion on the kind of questions to ask in an interview—whether it be a written or a personal interview. Students must decide what they want to know about the person and then develop questions that elicit that information.

COURT REPORTERS, CLERKS AND BAILIFFS

Objective: **Students will be able to explain the importance of an accurate transcript of a trial.**

Students will be able to explain one responsibility of a clerk and a bailiff.

Lawyers and judges are not the only people necessary for a trial. In addition, there are clerks, bailiffs, and court reporters.

The COURT REPORTER takes down all that happens during a trial. That includes all the questions asked by the lawyers, all the responses of the witnesses, and all the statements of the judge, including instructions to the jury. Because court reporters often take down as much as 250 words per minute, they usually use special machines that look like small typewriters on stilts. If the case is appealed to a higher court, the court reporter types his or her shorthand into words which read like a script. This script is called a transcript. Judges in an appeals court read the transcript to find out what happened during the trial.

What do you think is the reason for making a written record of what happens at a trial?

Consider the following situation:

Cynthia was found guilty of stealing a car.

After the hearing was over, everyone remembered her testimony differently.

Cynthia: I remember saying that I just went for a ride in my friend's car.

Her Lawyer: I remember her saying that she went for a ride with her friends and they told her the car was stolen.

The Police Officer: I remember her admitting that she and her friends stole the car together.

Does it make any difference whether Cynthia, the lawyer, or the police officer is right?

What difference does it make?

Would it help the appeals court to have a record of exactly what Cynthia said? How?

Note to teacher: In making a decision in a case, the judge or jury can rely only on evidence which is in the record. Therefore, with a written record, it is possible to challenge a decision which is against the weight of evidence. Thus, in Cynthia's case if the transcript shows that most of the testimony stated that Cynthia did not know the car was stolen, she might challenge the conviction. It should be noted that a challenge to a conviction is unlikely to be successful if the challenge is based on only one or two statements which are inconsistent with the conviction.

A case can be appealed on many different grounds, including: mistake of the judge in admitting or not admitting evidence, decision which is not supported by the evidence, statements by the judge or prosecutor likely to prejudice the jury, jury impanelled improperly, and other procedural irregularities.

One man was on trial for murder. The jury found him guilty. The man and his lawyer appealed, saying the judge made certain statements which were against the man during the trial and which influenced the jury. Why would a transcript help the appeals court decide whether this defendant was denied due process?

Without the special training in the use of the machine or in some cases, shorthand, it would be impossible to be a court reporter. A court reporter must take down everything that is said in the courtroom VERBATIM—word for word. It is possible to understand more about the job of a court reporter by seeing how well you can record words people are saying. . .

The following exercise can show you how many words a minute you can take down correctly.

You can make up your own abbreviations and spelling in order to write faster. Have one person be a witness and another be a lawyer. They can read the script on page 70. No one else should look at the script. One person should be the time-keeper. Everyone else in class should take down everything that is said as fast as possible. Try to keep straight who is speaking. After the testimony is over, write out in longhand what you recorded. Count the number of words you recorded. Divide this number by how many minutes the questioning took. Then, compare the different transcripts that students wrote. How would these different transcripts change the meaning of the testimony? After you have compared the different transcripts, turn to page 70 and compare them with the original script.

Note to teacher: In the debriefing you could help students see whether they were able to take down the important information correctly by asking questions such as:

1. What was the name of the witness?
2. Where was she employed?
3. What was the date the lawyers asked her about?
4. What was she doing on that date?
5. How long had she worked there?

After each question, if there are different answers to that question, discuss with the class whether it makes a difference what the correct information is.

Court reporters have proven excellent resources. Generally, there is some opportunity to speak with one at a field trip to the courts. Often there is a swing court reporter who fills in when a reporter is on vacation, or ill, or putting a final transcript together. Sometimes it is possible to have a court reporter come to a class. Several teachers have asked court reporters to give a demonstration with student attorneys asking questions. Court reporters will demonstrate their skills by having the students ask each other questions and then reading the information back to them from their machine. Discuss court reporters versus recording machines and the skills needed to become a court reporter. From listening to a court reporter students can gain appreciation for language arts skills, the ability to concentrate, patience and perserverance.

EXERCISE FOR STUDENT COURT REPORTERS

Lawyer: What is your name?

Mrs. Smith: Geraldine Smith.

Lawyer: Where are you employed Mrs. Smith?

Mrs. Smith: I am employed at the Harland Hardware Store.

Lawyer: What were you doing on January 19, 1980?

Mrs. Smith: I was at work as I had been every weekday for forty years.

Lawyer: Mrs. Smith, describe what happened at work on January 19, 1980.

Mrs. Smith: I was behind the cash register, I am the cashier. A man came up and asked for change for five dollars to use our pay phone. I gave him the change. Another man accidently hit this man with a rake that he was carrying out of the store. The first man yelled at the second man and then hit him in the nose.

Lawyer: Can you identify the man who asked for change and hit the second man?

Mrs. Smith: I can.

Lawyer: Is that man sitting in the court?

Mrs. Smith: He is and he is sitting in the defendant's seat.

Lawyer: What did the second man do when the first man hit him?

Mrs. Smith: He fell to the floor.

Lawyer: Mrs. Smith, could you describe how he fell?

Mrs. Smith: He fell very hard and struck his head on some glass bottles of cleaning solution.

Lawyer: What did the man do when he hit his head?

Mrs. Smith: He didn't move. There was blood all over his head.

MORE COURT PERSONNEL

The CLERK is also important in the court process.   All evidence
and all written papers of any kind are marked by the clerk.
It is the clerk who makes certain that the trial runs smoothly and
that all witnesses, evidence, and papers are in place.   In some
courts, the clerk also swears in the witnesses.

The BAILIFF keeps order in the courtroom.   The bailiff an-
nounces the opening of a trial, takes charge of the defendant in
criminal cases, and also looks after the jury members.   In some
courts, the bailiff might swear in the witnesses.

You will learn much more about all the jobs of court personnel
when you take part in your own mock trial.

Interested in knowing more about possible careers in the legal profession? There are many possibilities: legal secretaries, lawyers, court reporters, paralegals, legal assistants to name a few.

A good place to begin your research is in your school or local public library. The librarian can help you find one of the helpful books about careers in law. One that you might want to read is: *Careers in the Legal Profession* by Elinor Porter Swiger.

In addition, there are professional organizations with both national and local offices which have information about the kind of work their members do. For an updated list of addresses of the organizations write to West Publishing Company, Law in Action, Box T, 170 Old Country Road, Mineola, NY 11501.

LEGAL ASSISTANT OR PARALEGAL is a person who assists a lawyer in investigating facts, does legal research, and helps prepare documents. Paralegals can help lawyers in many ways, and they are employed in law firms all over the country.

LEGAL SECRETARIES are essential to a law firm. They must not only be excellent typists and take shorthand (or use a dictating machine) rapidly, but must know legal terms and how they apply. A knowledge of many medical terms and familiarity with legal documents is also necessary.

COURT REPORTERS are responsible for taking verbatim testimony in a trial. Court reporters work for the courts. Some are also employed as free lance people who do work for law firms.

LAWYERS are licensed by the state. To be licensed they must usually graduate from law school (although several states accept training in a law office instead of law school study). Then they must pass the bar examination in the state where they want to practice.

There are many kinds of lawyers. Some are in general practice and handle all kinds of cases. Others may specialize in a particular area. One source lists 34 different areas in which lawyers practice, and there are more. In addition, lawyers may work for the government, for large corporations, or for public service agencies.

We have suggested just a few of the careers which are open in the legal profession. If you are interested in knowing more about any one of them, there are many sources of information available to you. In addition to looking in your library for current books about the legal profession you could:

• Look in the Yellow Pages of your telephone directory. Under the heading "Schools, Secretarial or Business" you will find schools for legal secretaries and court reporters listed. A phone call to a school would give you the information you need about the length and cost of the course and previous educational requirements. (Most business schools require that you have a high school diploma or the high school equivalency certificate.)

• Contact the community college in your area. Many of them offer a course of training to become a paralegal or legal assistant. The course description which they send you will provide additional useful information.

• The national association of court reporters, legal secretaries, paralegals, or legal assistants, can probably give you more information about those jobs. You might write them.

• The American Bar Association, Circulation Department, 1155 East 60th Street, Chicago, IL 60637, has several helpful pamphlets. You could write to them. To learn more about becoming a lawyer you might call the law school in your city. If there isn't one in your community, write to the law school at your state university.

After you have checked the sources listed above you may still have some questions about the career that interests you which only a person working in that field could answer. If this happens, there are resource persons for law-related careers in your community that you could talk with. However before you call a busy law office or other resource person, do your home work. Work as a committee and assign specific tasks. Check the material available in your library. Write out your questions and then re-read them to be sure that they will help you get the information you really want. The resource person, even if the person is a friend of the family, will be more interested in talking with you if he/she sees that you have made some preparation for the interview. And, you will probably learn more because you will have some background information.

BEING A JUROR

Objective: **Students will be able to explain how jurors are selected.**

Students will be able to identify fact from opinion.

THE UNITED STATES CONSTITUTION SAYS:

Amendment

An accused person has the right to a speedy and public trial, by an impartial jury of the state and district wherein the crime shall have been committed.

Amendment

In civil cases the right to trial by jury shall be preserved.

Any United States citizen who is of legal age (18 or over or 21 or over, depending on the state) can be summoned to serve on a jury providing he/she has not been convicted of a serious crime (a felony).

UNITED STATES DISTRICT COURT
FOR THE
_____

SUMMONS FOR PETIT JUROR

To _____
_____

You are hereby summoned to appear in the United States District Court for the _____ District of _____ at Room _____ in the United States Courthouse, at _____ in City of _____ on _____ 19___, at _____ o'clock _____, to serve as a petit juror during a term of the court to commence on that day

By Order of the Court

_____
Clerk

Dated _____ 19___   By _____
Deputy

Why do you think the law requires people to serve on juries?

Note to teacher: A call to the jury commissioner or chief clerk of courts will answer your questions about who is exempt from jury duty in your state. You can also find out if there is a booklet available for people serving on jury duty. Often the jury commissioner or the court clerk will send you a copy of the brochure and a copy of the jury forms as well if you ask for them.
A very time-consuming but rewarding community involvement project is provided in the teacher's edition on page 153. The project involves developing (or rewriting an existing) "Instructions To The Jurors" booklet.

Not everyone who is summoned for jury duty has to serve. The following form shows the categories of persons who may be excused from jury duty in one state. Your state may allow other exemptions.

YOU MAY BE EXCUSED BY THE COURT FROM SERVICE AS A JUROR IF YOU FALL WITHIN A CATE- GORY LISTED HERE. MARK THAT EXCUSE WHICH APPLIES TO YOU IF YOU DEMAND TO BE EXCUSED FOR THAT REASON	☐ OVER 70 YEARS OF AGE ☐ AN ACTIVELY ENGAGED MINISTER OF RELIGION, OR MEMBER OF A RELIGIOUS ORDER OF ANY DENOMINATION. ☐ AN ACTIVELY PRACTICING ATTORNEY, PHYSICIAN, DENTIST, OR REGISTERED NURSE. ☐ A PERSON WHO HAS SERVED AS A GRAND OR PETIT JUROR IN STATE OR FEDERAL COURT WITHIN THE LAST TWO YEARS. (GIVE NAME OF COURT AND DATES YOU SERVED BELOW.)	☐ ACTIVELY ENGAGED IN A REGULARLY ES- TABLISHED PUBLIC, PAROCHIAL OR PRIVATE SCHOOL OR COLLEGE AS A TEACHER. ☐ SELF-EMPLOYED IN A "ONE-MAN" BUSINESS. ☐ RESIDING AT A DISTANCE OF MORE THAN 65 MILES ONE WAY FROM THE U.S. COURTHOUSE LOCATED AT ADDRESS SHOWN IN BOX 2 ABOVE. ☐ A PERSON WHO IS ESSENTIAL TO THE CARE OF CHILDREN OF TENDER YEARS OR OF AGED OR INFIRM PERSONS (EXPLAIN AND GIVE THEIR AGES BELOW.) ☐ ALL FULL TIME STUDENTS.

1. Do you agree that persons in each of the categories listed above should be excused from serving on a jury? Why? Why not?

2. Do you think other categories of people should be excused? Explain.

3. Do you think people should be able to get out of serving on a jury if they just don't want to? Explain your answer.

People who are called to jury duty meet in the jury waiting room at the courthouse. They are picked at random to go to a particular trial.

What does it mean to be picked at random? Why do you think this way is used?

More prospective jurors are assigned to a case than are actually needed to make up the jury. The persons who will serve on the jury are chosen from this group. The lawyers on each side will question each potential jury member to find out if they want that person on the jury. This questioning is called VOIR DIRE —French words which mean "see and say" (the truth).

Here are some questions lawyers might ask prospective jurors during the VOIR DIRE.

The prosecutor might ask:

> Do you have any knowledge of this crime from reading newspapers?

> Do you have any religious or moral beliefs that would keep you from returning a guilty verdict?

The defense lawyer might ask:

> Do you believe that if a person is charged with a crime he or she is guilty?

> Are you more willing to believe a police officer than another witness simply because he or she is a police officer?

Explain why the lawyers would ask each of these questions.

Lawyers can strike (remove) a certain number of people from the list of prospective jurors. Once chosen as a jury member for a case, the person has a duty to make a decision based on the facts of the case. The lawyers and judge leave it up to the jury to determine what actually happened, based on the facts presented, and to reach a decision based on those facts and on the instructions on the law which the judge gives them at the end of the case.

Note to teacher: It should be clear to the students that the purpose of questioning is to select *unbiased* jurors. Questions to jurors may cover specific prejudices, such as prejudices based on race, age, sex, or religion, and may seek to discover whether the juror might have any monetary interest in the case.

Sometimes it is difficult for jurors to tell the difference between facts and opinions in statements made during a trial. Read the following statements. Decide which are *facts* and which are *opinions*. Be careful, it is easy to confuse the two.

"She couldn't have done it because...

She's too nice a person." (Opinion)

She was with me on that day." (Fact)

She couldn't reach the latch." (Fact)

She is too smart to do something that stupid." (Opinion)

She was in the hospital on that day." (Fact)

FACTS to KNOW

1. Only witnesses can give evidence during a trial.

2. In a criminal trial the prosecutor must prove that the defendant is guilty "beyond a reasonable doubt."

3. In civil cases proof beyond a reasonable doubt is not necessary rather, there must be "a preponderance of the evidence," which means "more likely than not."

What could you do to help potential jurors understand how important their job is?

One idea is to make posters for the jury waiting room.   Here are some examples:

Where would our Court system be without JURORS?	Rm. 211 at Bancroft School is glad you are a RESPONSIBLE CITIZEN. Thank you for being a JURY MEMBER.

Another way you might show that you care about the work they are doing is to bring in magazines or books for the jury room. Ask the jury commissioner about this idea.   Another idea is to have your class donate money to buy a magazine subscription for the jury room.   A sign could be placed in the jury room explaining your gift and thanking the people for being jurors.

Or, contact the jury commissioner by phone or letter.   Explain that you would like to do a project to support the jury system. Ask the jury commissioner for suggestions for how your class could help.

BEING A WITNESS

Objective: **Students will be able to explain two reasons why a witness is a vital part of the court system.**

Students will discuss problems involved in being a witness.

We have studied the responsibilities of lawyers, judges, and jurors to make sure the trial is fair. But. . .

WHAT ABOUT WITNESSES? HOW DO THEY MAKE THE COURTS WORK?

A person accused of a crime has a right to:

—confront and cross-examine witnesses

—call in witnesses to speak on his/her behalf

A person who is a witness upholds the right of a defendant in a criminal trial to hear the charge against him/her and to have people speak on his/her behalf.

RIGHTS

People in society have a right to:

—be protected from law-breakers by having suspected law-breakers stand trial.

A person who is a witness also upholds the right of people in society to be protected from law-breakers by reporting what he/she knows about the facts of a case.

BUT
People sometimes react to being a witness in this way:

"I can't take time away from my work to go to court and be a witness. I'm sure other people saw it happen too. I don't want to get involved in it anyway!"

Look at these pictures.   What information might these citizens have that could be important in a trial?

When a person is a witness that person testifies to (tells about) what he or she has seen or heard or knows.   Experts are often asked to be witnesses in trials to explain certain information they know which is important to the case.   In what types of cases might a medical doctor be asked to be a witness?   How about a ballistics (fire arms) specialist?   A tax auditor?

Read the next three stories about witnesses and answer the questions that follow. As you read the stories be thinking about the question: Should citizens volunteer to testify as witnesses?

Story 1

What if you were arrested for vandalizing a building? The police found one witness who identified you as one of the vandals. You happened to be walking in the area near the building but you did not vandalize it. You saw some neighbors out in their yards who must have seen the real vandals. None of these people told the police what they saw.

How would you feel?

If your case came to trial and none of the witnesses testified, do you think you could get a fair trial?

Explain in your own words why witnesses are important in order to have a fair trial.

Story 2

What if Amanda witnessed her neighbor severely beat a five-year-old child on more than one occasion? She finally reported the incidents to the police. She was subpoenaed to be a witness at the neighbor's trial. Amanda spent half of a workday in the office of the prosecuting lawyer preparing the case, then she spent one more workday in court during the trial.

Amanda was a secretary in a small business and having her away from the office made it difficult for the business to run smoothly. Her boss was upset and Amanda got no pay for the days she didn't work.

If you were Amanda how would you have handled the situation?

Do you agree or disagree with how Amanda's boss acted? If you knew Amanda's boss, what could you say to him or her about how he or she acted? What are your reasons?

The court has the power to subpoena witnesses.

A subpoena requires that the witness appear in court on a certain day. The witness can be arrested if he or she does not obey the subpoena. Because of the Fifth Amendment protection against self-incrimination, the witness does not have to answer questions even though he or she must appear in court.

Explain why you agree or disagree with the law that says witnesses must appear in court.

In some states there is a small witness fee paid for every day that the witness is in court, but it may not be as much as a day's wages. Should it be against the law for any employer to discourage an employee from being a witness? What are the reasons for and against this law? What are the problems of a small business? What other things should you consider before making a decision?

Story 3

John saw a boy he recognized from school knock down old Mrs. Jones, his neighbor.   The boy stole Mrs. Jones' purse and ran away.   John watched Mrs. Jones pick herself up.   She did not seem to be hurt.   Just then a police car drove down the street and Mrs. Jones waved for it to stop.   Mrs. Jones told the police that she did not get a good look at the purse snatcher and she didn't think that there were any witnesses to the crime.   John didn't know what to do.   He wanted to help Mrs. Jones get her purse back but he was afraid to come forward and be a witness.

Why should John be a witness?   Think of as many reasons as you can.

Why should John walk away and not get involved?   Think of as many reasons as you can.

If you had been in John's shoes what do you think you might have done in this situation?   Why?

If you were a witness to any kind of crime or accident would you be—WILLING TO TESTIFY IN COURT?

Decide what your opinion is on this question and then take a stand on the opinion line. If you agree with No Witness Nancy, stand all the way to the left of the line. If you agree with Witness Willy, stand all the way to the right of the line. If your opinion falls somewhere in the middle, stand at the place on the line that best represents your opinion on this question. Give a reason to back up your opinion.

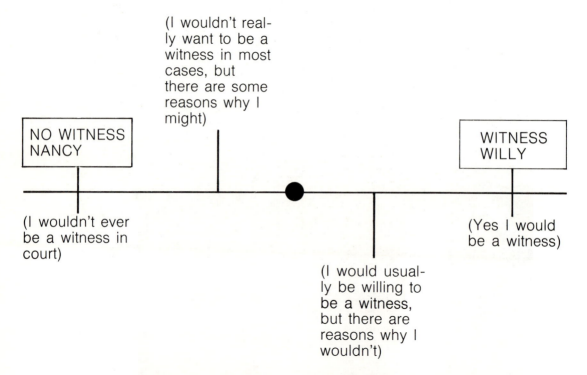

(I wouldn't real-
ly want to be a
witness in most
cases, but
there are some
reasons why I
might)

NO WITNESS
NANCY

WITNESS
WILLY

(I wouldn't ever
be a witness in
court)

(Yes I would
be a witness)

(I would usual-
ly be willing to
be a witness,
but there are
reasons why I
wouldn't)

Note to teacher: Students might take a stand on an opinion line that is written across a chalkboard. You might then interview the students to ask why they are standing where they are. Five or six students at a time work best at the opinion line. Alternatively, you might have everyone in the class come up to the chalkboard and write their names at the spot on the line that best represents their opinion. Students should give reasons to back up their opinions.

The fact that people are often afraid to be witnesses in a trial is a big problem for the courts. Many people don't know what laws exist to protect witnesses. Some police departments have special policies about protecting witnesses that people need to know about as well.

Find out if there are laws to protect witnesses in your state. You might write to your state representative or ask a lawyer to help you find state laws about protecting witnesses. Also, contact your police department to find out what they do to protect witnesses.

Put together the information you gather in a Fact Sheet. Distribute the fact sheets to families in your school or to people in your neighborhood.

86

Objective: Students will be able to define words introduced in Section II

attorney _____

evidence _____

hearsay _____

negotiate _____

sentence _____

subpoena _____

testify _____

transcript _____

voir dire _____

You've already seen these words in previous lessons. Do you know the meaning of them right now? See if you can say or write the meaning of these words. Can you do it? Check your definitions with the ones in the glossary to see if they are correct. Write the correct definition for any word you missed.

Find the words listed above in the box below.

Seek and Find*

T	O	A	H	S	C	T	I	P	S	A	T	O
E	V	L	Q	U	L	F	V	E	U	R	S	D
S	A	E	M	B	R	I	O	B	B	L	E	T
T	T	R	A	N	S	C	R	I	P	T	N	S
I	T	S	P	C	R	N	B	Z	O	D	T	E
F	O	A	E	R	N	L	I	F	E	B	E	V
Y	R	K	D	S	Y	A	H	X	N	A	N	I
P	N	F	U	R	A	M	K	I	A	S	C	D
N	E	G	O	T	I	A	T	E	R	L	E	E
S	Y	N	E	Y	B	C	T	I	Z	L	O	N
V	O	I	R	D	I	R	E	N	E	I	N	C
I	D	P	H	E	A	R	S	A	Y	H	K	E
T	P	N	I	C	H	Z	Y	M	I	X	E	L

*Copyright © Star-Telegram Syndicate, Inc. 1975

NEWSBULLETIN REVIEW—SECTION II

Objective: **Students will be able to answer questions on a class test about information presented in Section II.**

Note to students: This lesson is a review quiz. You can use it to check how much you have learned so far about courts and trials. Some classes have turned these reviews into newsbulletins. When your answers get printed in a newsbulletin, they help other people learn what you have learned.

Note to teacher: Have the students turn to the blank newsbulletin on the next page. The class may vote on the name or letterhead of the newsbulletin. Then, each student should complete every section of the newsbulletin by answering the questions or giving his/her opinion.

The newsbulletin technique can be used as the evaluation measure or test. The "best" articles can be printed on ditto masters and made to look like a real newspaper. The newsbulletin should stimulate the students to try hard to answer all the questions on the "test."

NEWSBULLETIN REVIEW

CROSSWORD PUZZLE

¹A	¹T	T	O	R	N	E	Y			
	R									
	A							³H		
	N			²V				E		
	²S	U	B	P	O	E	N	A		
	C			I				R		
	R			R				S		
	I			D				A		
	P			I				Y		
	T			R						
				E						

Across

1. A lawyer
2. A court paper ordering a witness to appear in court

Down

1. A written record of every word said at the trial.
2. Choosing a jury for a trial is called
3. A type of evidence not allowed at a trial.

EDITORIAL

Do you think witnesses are necessary in order to have a fair trial? Give reasons for your answer.

CARTOON

Draw a picture that would help some-one understand the skills lawyers need to act as negotiators. Or de-scribe in writing some of those skills.

ADVICE

Your friend receives a summons for jury duty. Your friend wants to get out of serving. What advice would you give your friend?

JOB RESPONSIBILITIES

Name one responsibility each of the following people have at a trial.

Judge _____

_____

Lawyers _____

_____

Court Reporter _____

_____

Jury Members _____

_____

SECTION III
IN MUNICIPAL COURT

Objective: **Students will become familiar with legal procedure for less serious offenses.**

Not everyone who commits a crime gets to have a trial even if he or she wants one. In many states a person who commits a less serious crime, such as speeding or disturbing the peace, will probably just appear before a judge without a jury. The Supreme Court has ruled that this is all right, but only when the penalty for the crime is less than six months in jail. At this type of trial the accused person is allowed to have a lawyer and is able to call witnesses to testify.

The case of Jimmie Smith tells the story of the legal steps a person who is accused of a less serious offense goes through.

THE CASE OF JIMMIE SMITH

Mr. and Mrs. Davis like to go to bed at nine o'clock. One summer night, their next door neighbor, Jimmie Smith, had a party. About 11 p.m. the Davises were awakened by people laughing and loud music coming from Jimmie's front porch. Mr. Davis got up and yelled, "You young hoodlums had better shut up or I'll call the police!" Jimmie yelled back, "Go back to bed old man, I have a right to have fun on my own front porch."

Mr. and Mrs. Davis tried to go back to sleep, but at 1 a.m. they were still awake because of the music and loud talking coming from Jimmie's place. Mr. Davis was mad because this wasn't the first time Jimmie Smith had disturbed them. Mr. Davis called the police. He complained that the party at Jimmie Smith's place was disturbing the peace.

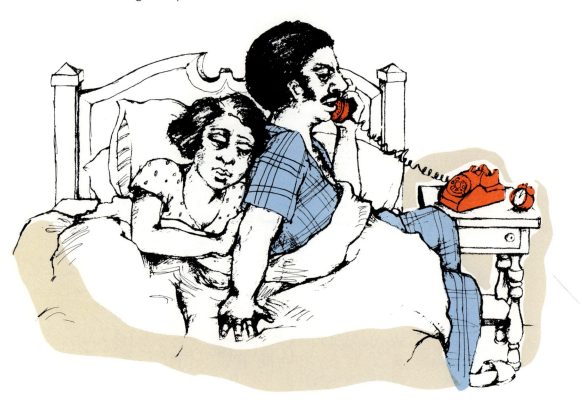

When the police arrived they asked Mr. Davis to fill out a complaint form like this one:

COMPLAINT

KANSAS CITY
vs.

Jimmie Smith

No. *4441 Main, Apt 4* Street

IN THE MUNICIPAL COURT OF
KANSAS CITY

DIVISION NO.

STATE OF MISSOURI, } ss.
County of Jackson

Mr. Henry Davis of No. *4441 Main, Apt 1* Street

being duly sworn, states on oath, that on or about the *2* day of *September* 19 *75*

at or near *4441 Main*

within the corporate limits of Kansas City, Mo., one *Jimmie Smith*

did then and there unlawfully *create unreasonably loud, disturbing, and unnecessary noise by playing a record player.*

in violation of the ordinances of said city.

Mr. Henry Davis
Complainant.

Subscribed and sworn to before me this *3 rd*

day of *September* 19 *75.*

John Doe
Assistant City Counselor.

QUESTIONS:

1. Why do you think the police wanted Mr. Davis to write down his complaint on paper?

2. Call the police station and ask if the name of a person making a complaint is always made known to the person charged with the violation.

3. Have you ever known anyone who wanted to make a complaint but did not want to fill out a form? Why do you think people sometimes do not want to fill out a form or put their complaint in writing?

Note to teacher: The students should give some ideas about the need for and advantages of a written statement of complaint, for example:

- it gives the law enforcement officer an account which he/she can easily refer back to.
- it assures accuracy.
- it prevents any accusations that police or other law enforcement officers are being unfair or trying "to get" someone.
- since it is a more involved process than a verbal complaint, a person making a complaint would not act hastily or just from a momentary anger.
- persons may be unwilling to file a written complaint for fear of retaliation.

Back to Jimmie Smith—

The police then went to Jimmie's apartment and told him that he was under arrest for violating a section of the city law stating that it is against the law to disturb the peace. The police took Jimmie to the police station where he was given a court summons and his bail was set at $25.00. Jimmie called a friend to come pay the $25.00 so he wouldn't have to spend the night in jail.

IN THE MUNICIPAL COURT OF KANSAS CITY, MISSOURI STATE OF MISSOURI, COUNTY OF JACKSON–CLAY–PLATTE SS				THE UNDERSIGNED COMPLAINS AND STATES THAT			STATION COPY OF INFORMATION NO.	G180007		
On or About 9/2/75	In Kansas City, Missouri 4441 Main		At or Near	At About (Time) 7 AM	Last Name Smith,	First Jimmie		Middle (none)		
Address 4441 Main Apt 4	City and State Kansas City, Mo.		Age 28	DOB 8/1/47	State of Birth Mo.	Race B	Sex M	Hgt 5'8"	Wgt 160	Eyes Br	Hair Bl
SSN	Employer Sears	Address 4500 Central		Relative Name Smith, Mary (Mo)			Address 3824 Main			

DID UNLAWFULLY WITHIN THE AFORESAID CITY, COUNTY AND STATE COMMIT THE FOLLOWING OFFENSE

Did create unreasonably loud, disturbing, and unnecessary noise by playing a record player.

In Violation of the Revised Ordinances of Kansas City, Missouri, 1966, As Amended, Chapter 26 Section 26.13 Penalty Chapter 1, Section 1.7

Above Complaint Is True As I Verily Believe

COMPLAINANT: Henry Davis OFFICER Arthur Jones Serial No. 2600 Unit CAP Pat. Area CCn

On information and upon official oath the prosecutor complains and informs the Court that these facts are true as he verily believes Ben , Assistant City Counselor Filed 9/4/75

Case Report Number 9000 Date, Time & Location Of Arrest If Other Than Above: Searched By

Bond No.	Bond Amount $25.00	Property No. 111	Court Date 9/30/75	Time 8:30	Place 1101 Locust Street	Room A	Without Admitting Guilt, I Promise to Appear in the Municipal Court of Kansas City, Missouri, At the Time Indicated Hereon Defendant's Signature Jimmie Smith

G180007

1. Where on the summons does it tell what law Jimmie was accused of breaking?

2. Where on the summons does it tell Jimmie when and where to appear in court?

Back to the Story—

The next day Jimmie talked to a lawyer and told him what had happened. Jimmie told the lawyer that he thought he was not guilty of disturbing the peace and he felt that the Davis couple were just old grouches who liked to complain about everything. Jimmie said he had a witness, Margaret Eagan, his other neighbor, who said that she was home all night and had not been disturbed by any noise.* The lawyer told Jimmie that he had several choices: he could defend himself, he could pay the lawyer to defend him on the day of his trial, or he could plead guilty to the charge and accept the sentence the judge gave him without a trial.

If you were in Jimmie's shoes, would you want to defend yourself in court?

Or would you decide to pay a lawyer to defend you?

Or would you just plead guilty and accept the penalty that the judge gave you?

Explain the reasons for your decision.

*The lawyer told Jimmie that he could subpoena Mrs. Eagan to testify on his behalf in court.

94

PREPARATION FOR A JURY TRIAL

Objective: Students will become familiar with legal procedure involved in having a case tried by a jury.

From Beginning to End of a Legal Case

The steps necessary to reach a court decision in a case can be long and complex. These steps are explained in this lesson.

> **Note to teacher:** Students usually look at a mock trial as just the act of putting on the trial. This lesson is basically a reading lesson which provides students the step by step procedure needed to prepare and execute a trial. To make this lesson more action-oriented you could ask 17 students to read one step each and paraphrase that step so that it can be presented to the rest of the class. Another way is to have one student read it and another student paraphrase what that person read.

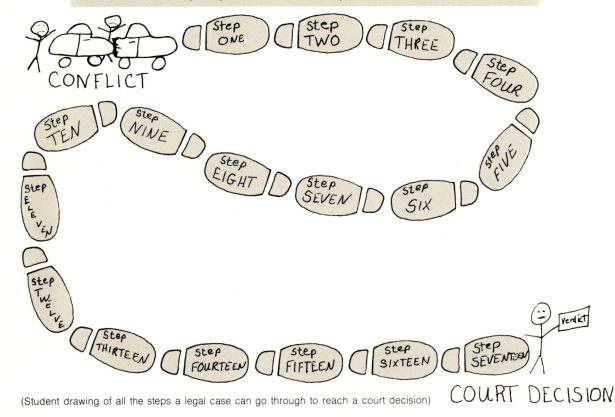

(Student drawing of all the steps a legal case can go through to reach a court decision)

Step 1
Legal Conflict

There is a conflict that can be decided by taking it to court. (Not all conflicts can be decided by courts of law.) In criminal cases, the conflict is between the government and the person accused of committing a crime.

In civil cases the lawyers try to settle the conflict without having to go the court. If this doesn't work, the person with the complaint can decide to take it to court.

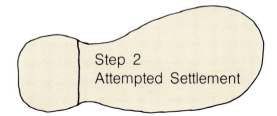

Step 2
Attempted Settlement

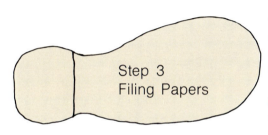

Step 3
Filing Papers

In civil cases a paper called a *complaint* is filed in court which describes the plaintiffs claim against the defendant. The defendant's lawyer can then file an *answer* which denies the complaint in some way. In criminal cases the pleading is called an *indictment*. It states the government's charge or a complaint against the defendant.

Lawyers get all the facts by interviewing witnesses and examining evidence (such as x-rays, or medical bills). They may go to the scene of the crime or accident. Sworn statements witnesses make before a trial in response to lawyer's questions are called *depositions*. There are certain rules lawyers must follow when taking depositions.

Step 4
Lawyers Get Facts

Step 5
Lawyers Prepare for Trial

Lawyers decide which facts are important to bring out at the trial and prepare questions that will get witnesses to testify about those facts. The lawyers usually go over the questions with their witnesses before the trial.

Criminal trials must occur within a short time (30–60 days) after indictment, because of the constitutional right to a speedy trial (Sixth Amendment). It usually takes several months to a year for a civil case requiring a jury trial to come to court. To open the court, the bailiff calls the court to order. The judge comes in and the name of the case is announced.

Step 6
Trial Begins

Step 7
The Voir Dire

More than 12 jury members are chosen for every case. During the *voir dire* the lawyers ask the jury members questions and decide which jury candidates they want as jurors on that case.

The plaintiff's lawyer (or the prosecutor) gives the opening statement first. The defense lawyer can make his/her opening statement at that time or just before questioning his/her witnesses. In the opening statement each lawyer tells the jury his/her client's side of the story and argues that it is the one to be believed.

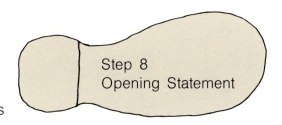

Step 8
Opening Statement

Step 9
Direct Examination
by Plaintiff's Lawyer

Plaintiff's lawyer (or prosecutor) calls his/her witness(es) to the stand first. The lawyer asks the witnesses questions to bring out facts which are favorable to the plaintiff's (or prosecution's) case. The lawyer also presents physical evidence and asks the witness who knows about it to identify it.

After direct examination of each witness for the plaintiff (or prosecution), the lawyer for the defendant cross-examines by asking the witness more questions to bring out facts which are favorable to the defendant or which show that the witness is unsure, confused, or not telling the truth in his/her testimony.

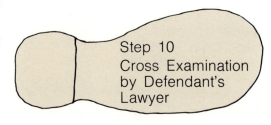

Step 10
Cross Examination
by Defendant's
Lawyer

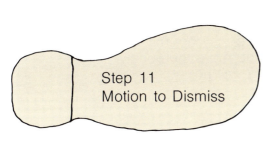

Step 11
Motion to Dismiss

After all of the plaintiff's (or prosecution's) witnesses have testified and all of the evidence has been presented, the defendant's lawyer may ask the court to dismiss the case, or throw it out of court. If the judge thinks that all of the plaintiff's evidence was not enough to prove his/her case, the judge will dismiss the case. That would be the end of the trial. However, few cases are dismissed. Usually judges go ahead with the trial and ask the defendant to try to support his/her side of the case.

The defendant's lawyer calls the defense witnesses to the stand and asks questions to bring out facts which are favorable to the defendant. The lawyer also presents physical evidence favorable to the defendant and asks a witness who knows about it to identify it.

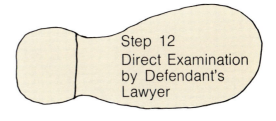

Step 12
Direct Examination
by Defendant's
Lawyer

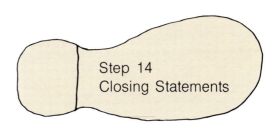

Step 13
Cross Examination
by Plaintiff's Lawyer

The plaintiff's lawyer (or prosecutor) may cross examine each of these witnesses for the defense by asking them specific questions which might bring out facts favorable to the plaintiff (or prosecution) or which might show they are unsure, confused, or not telling the truth in their testimony.

After all the testimony has been heard, each lawyer makes a short speech to the jury. First, the plaintiff's lawyer (or prosecuting attorney) speaks. Then, the defendant's lawyer gets a turn. Both lawyers sum up facts that have been brought out during the trial which support their side of the story. They try hard to convince the jury to believe their side of the story.

Step 14
Closing Statements

Note to teacher: If the judge rather than a jury is deciding a case, the lawyers make the closing statements to the judge. The judge will usually make a decision on the case then. However, in complicated civil cases, the judge may not make a decision until he/she considers the evidence more thoroughly. In a judge-tried case, steps 7 and 15–17 will not occur.

Step 15
Judge Instructs the Jury

After the closing statements, the judge reads instructions to the jury about the law applicable to the case.

The jury leaves the courtroom and is taken by the bailiff to a private room where they will make their decision. Their decision is called a *verdict*.

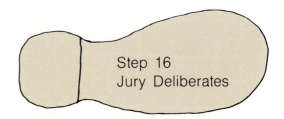

Step 16
Jury Deliberates

Step 17
Reading the Verdict

The jury returns to the courtroom. The jury foreperson reads the *verdict* to the judge. The trial is then over. (In criminal cases, the bailiff takes charge of the defendant if he/she is found guilty.)

You have learned the steps in putting on a trial, now **you** can put on a

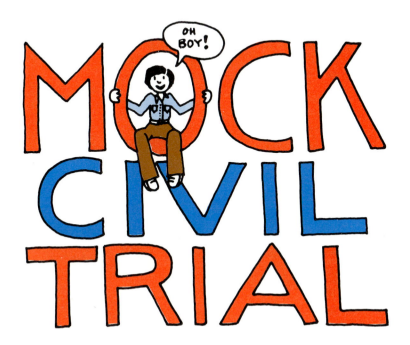

or a

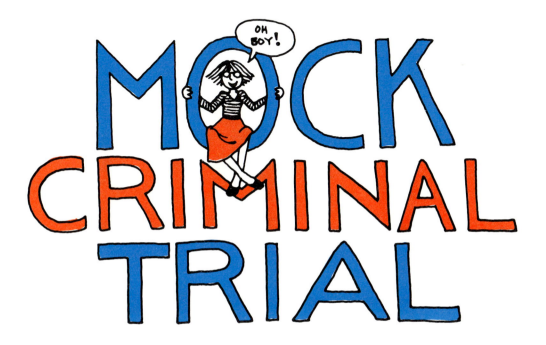

NOTES TO TEACHER ON PUTTING ON A MOCK TRIAL

The purpose of having the students enact their own mock trial is to have them learn basic court procedure and understand through experience what it feels like to be the various people in a courtroom drama.

Roles: *Lawyers.* Allow students to choose who they want to be in the trial or, if you prefer, assign roles. The number of students portraying lawyers depends upon how the trial tasks are divided within each lawyer group. In the civil mock trial, there are 8 tasks to be performed by each side during the trial:

A. Voir dire
B. Opening statement
C. Closing statement
D. Examination of plaintiff
E. Examination of defendant
F. Examination of Doctor Perkins
G. Examination of Officer MacArthur
H. Examination of Henry Oliver

With 2 students, the relative difficulty and variability of the tasks suggest dividing responsibilities as follows:

Student #1: A, C, E, F
Student #2: B, D, G, H

With 3 students, task suggest dividing as follows

Student #1: A, F, G
Student #2: B, D, H
Student #3: E, C

With 4 students, the tasks may be divided as follows:
Student #1: A, G
Student #2: B, E
Student #3: D, H
Student #4: C, F

Because the tasks assigned to students portraying lawyers call for a substantial written work product, you may consider giving these students extra credit for their work or exempting them from another assignment.

Jury. More than 12 students can be in the jury work group so that 12 may be selected in the voir dire.

Jury selection: The mock trial script and instructions include voir dire (jury selection). Voir dire is a very time-consuming process in a real trial and could result in lengthening a mock trial beyond the limits of your class period. There are several ways to handle it: Schedule the voir dire and the opening of the trial to take place on the day before the rest of the trial. Students who have visited a real trial will recognize that getting a trial started may take several days because of jury selection. Alternatively, the voir dire can be eliminated from the script and the students instructed to assume voir dire has been performed. In such a case, it would be a good idea to allow the entire class to participate in voir dire as a class exercise. A compromise solution is to include the voir dire but limit the number of questions which can be asked. *Decide* on how jury selection will be treated at the beginning so the lawyers and the bailiff will know whether to prepare for voir dire.

If you decide to include voir dire, instruct each lawyer responsible for voir dire how many jury candidates he/she can strike (remove) from the list in selecting the jury. Most juries have 12 members, some have 6, but you may want more students to participate in the process. The number each lawyer can strike is half the number of excess candidates over the number you want on the jury. Students who are not selected for the jury by the lawyers should be asked to be court observers who will critique participants during the debriefing.

Time limits: If you are concerned that the mock trial be limited to one class period, it is a good idea to establish time limits for the various components of the trial so that all parts of the trial will be covered. The court clerk can be responsible for seeing that the time limits are followed.

Witnesses: Students should recognize that every participant in a trial is important to its success. Thus, if a witness is sick and unable to attend the trial when it is scheduled, often a trial will be rescheduled for another day, even after all the other participants—the judge and other court officers, the lawyers, and the witnesses are present. One way to demonstrate this graphically—if you can tolerate the chaos likely to result and you can arrange for your law student to return—is to reschedule the trial if one of the students playing a lawyer or witness is absent from school. If all the students are present, which is likely to be the case on the day of a mock trial, arrange to have one of the witnesses summoned to the principal's office for the class period. Students should discuss why the trial was cancelled and their feelings about it being cancelled. How do you think participants in real trials feel when trials are cancelled?

Examination of a witness by both lawyers may be repeated several times before a witness is excused. The lawyer who called a witness to testify has the right to question the witness again after cross-examination (re-direct) in order to ask about information brought out during the cross-examination. After this, the opposing lawyer may cross-examine the witness again (re-cross). This process may be repeated several times. Before the trial, settle on "rules" for how many times a lawyer may examine a witness.

MOCK CIVIL TRIAL

Objective: Students will participate in a mock civil trial.

Case Summary: *Richards v. Dinkins*

On the night of January 2, 1980, an accident occurred at the corner of Lindell and Taylor Avenue at about 11:20 p.m. Mrs. Didi Richards was driving west on Lindell Street in a Volkswagen when she was hit by a Chevy Nova which Mrs. Charlotte Dinkins was driving north on Taylor. There are yellow flashing lights on Lindell for traffic going east and west, and there are red flashing lights on Taylor. The accident occurred when Mrs. Richards' car was midway through the intersection. Mrs. Richards was thrown across the seat by the crash.

Soon after the accident Police Officer MacArthur arrived on the scene. He took down the names of the two women and asked what happened. Each woman said that the accident was not her fault. The police officer saw a passerby who had witnessed the accident and questioned him. Officer MacArthur took Mrs. Richards to the hospital where she was treated for a broken wrist. Mrs. Dinkins went home without assistance.

One week after the accident Mrs. Richards complained of back and neck pains. She had also learned that the damage to her car amounted to $800. She tried to get Mrs. Dinkins to pay for the damage to her car and for her injuries, but Mrs. Dinkins refused to pay. Mrs. Richards decided to see a lawyer about the case. Mrs. Richards and her lawyer decided to sue Mrs. Dinkins for $4,000 in damages, plus court costs.

Before filing a lawsuit, Mrs. Richards' lawyer wrote to Mrs. Dinkins to give her a chance to pay for Mrs. Richards' injuries and damages without a suit. Mrs. Dinkins refused to pay anything. Then the lawyer wrote a PETITION, or legal complaint, against Mrs. Dinkins and filed it at the trial court. In her complaint, Mrs. Richards said that the accident was caused by Mrs. Dinkins because she didn't stop at a red light, she didn't look for other cars, and she didn't have her car under control. In this case, Mrs. Richards is the PLAINTIFF and Mrs. Dinkins is the DEFENDANT.

Note to teacher: In a real case, the defendant (here, Mrs. Dinkins) might file a counterclaim against the plaintiff (Mrs. Richards) for her injuries and damages to her car. For the sake of simplicity in presenting the mock trial, we have not posed such a situation in these materials.

Here is the petition (complaint) Mrs. Richards' lawyer filed:

General Trial Court of _____
(your state)

Didi Richards,
      Plaintiff
    v.
Charlotte Dinkins,
      Defendant.

PETITION

Comes now the plaintiff and states that:

1.   Plaintiff is a resident of the State of _____ residing at 1215 (your state) Walnut Street in _____ .
(your city)   (your state)

2.   Defendant is a resident and citizen of the State of _____ (your state) residing at 1117 Main Street in _____ .
(your city)

3.   On the 2nd day of January, 1980, while plaintiff was driving west on Lindell Street in _____, her Volkswagen automobile was struck in a (your city) collision with a Chevrolet Nova automobile operated by the defendant in a northerly direction on Taylor Street.

4.   Said collision was caused by negligence on the part of the defendant in the following manner:

in failing to stop the Chevrolet automobile at a red traffic signal;

in failing to exercise the highest degree of care to keep a lookout for persons and vehicles upon the street; and

in failing to have the Chevrolet automobile under control.

5.   As a result of said collision and negligence of defendant, plaintiff was injured in the following ways: a broken wrist; bruises over arms and legs; tense and nervous condition; back and neck pains, all to the damage of $3,200 and plaintiff's automobile was damaged in the sum of $800.

Wherefore, plaintiff prays for judgment against defendant in the total sum of $4,000 and her costs.

_____
Lawyer for Plaintiff
321 Chestnut Street

When Mrs. Dinkins learned that she was being sued, she went to her lawyer and told her side of the story. She felt the accident was not her fault and she shouldn't have to pay Mrs. Richards anything. Mrs. Dinkins' lawyer filed an *Answer* at the trial court. In her *Answer*, Mrs. Dinkins admitted that the accident happened, but she said that it was not her fault.

It will be up to you to have the trial for Mrs. Richards and Mrs. Dinkins.

One judge
Two plaintiff's lawyers
Two defendant's lawyers
One court reporter
One bailiff
One clerk
Jury members
Charlotte Dinkins
Didi Richards
Officer MacArthur
Henry Oliver
Dr. Perkins

Students should work together in the groups specified below to prepare for the trial. The students should understand the information and follow the directions given in their work group sheets.

Group 1. Witnesses, Charlotte Dinkins, and Didi Richards pages 134–136
Group 2. Plaintiff's attorneys pages 139; 141–144
Group 3. Defendant's attorneys pages 140; 141–144
Group 4. Judge, court reporter pages 145–146
Group 5. Clerk, bailiff pages 147–148
Group 6. Jury pages 149–152

JURY MEMBERS: DO NOT READ ANY MORE ABOUT THE CASE OF *RICHARDS v. DINKINS!*

Note to teacher: Be sure to read note to teacher on pages 132 and 133 for more information on how to prepare for the trial.

COURT PROCEDURE FOR A

MOCK CIVIL TRIAL

Note to teacher: In actual trials, the witnesses may be kept outside the courtroom until they are called to the stand so that they don't hear the testimony of the other witnesses. You may decide whether or not you wish to follow this procedure.

 OPENING OF THE COURT

(The bailiff rises and says in a loud, clear voice:)

Bailiff: "All rise. The court of _____ is now open and in session, the Honorable Judge _____ presiding.

(The judge enters. Everyone rises and remains standing until the judge sits down.)

Bailiff: "All persons having business before the court may now approach the bench."

Judge: "The case of _____. Is the plaintiff ready?"

Plaintiff's lawyer: "The plaintiff is ready."

Judge: "Is the defendant ready?"

Defendant's lawyer: "The defendant is ready."

 JURY SELECTION

Judge: "Let's proceed with the jury selection. Does the plaintiff have any questions to ask the candidates?"

Plaintiff's lawyer: (Begin questions to jury candidates. When you finish, say: That is all, Your Honor.")

Judge: "Does the defendant have any questions to ask the jury candidates?"

Defendant's lawyer: (Begin questions to jury candidates. When you finish, say: "That is all, Your Honor.")

Judge: "We will now have a one minute recess while the lawyers decide on the jurors." (After a minute, say: "Lawyers, are you ready?")

All lawyers: "Yes, Your Honor."

Judge: "Then, proceed."

Plaintiff's lawyer: "Plaintiff strikes _____,

_____, _____,_____

(Give all names of jury candidates you do not want.)

Defendant's lawyer: "Defendant strikes _____,

_____, _____,_____

(Give all names of jury candidates you do not want.)

Bailiff: (Lead the candidates who will not be on the jury away from the jury area.)

Judge: "It is now time to swear in the jury."

Clerk: (Swears in all jury members at one time.) "The jury will rise, raise your right hands and be sworn in.

> Do you solemnly swear that you will well and truly try the issues now to be given to you; that you will speak nothing to anyone of the business or matters you have in hand, nor will you let anyone speak to you about the same but in court and when you are agreed upon any verdict, you will keep it secret until you deliver it up in court? Do you all so swear?"

Jury: (All together) "I do."

Clerk: "You may be seated."

 OPENING STATEMENTS

Judge: "Does the plaintiff have an opening statement?"

Plaintiff's lawyer: (rise) "Yes, Your Honor." (Make opening statement, then sit down.)

Judge: "Does the defendant have an opening statement?"

Defendant's lawyer: (rise) "Yes, Your Honor." (Make opening statement, then sit down.)

EXAMINATION OF PLAINTIFF'S WITNESSES

Judge: "Plaintiff, call your first witness."

Plaintiff's lawyer: (rises) "_____"

(name of first witness)

Clerk: "First witness, _____, shall take the stand." (The clerk should swear in each witness before he/she testifies. When the swearing in is finished, say to the witness: "Please be seated.")

Plaintiff's lawyer: (Begin direct examination of witness.)

Judge: "Does the defendant wish to cross-examine this witness?"

Defendant's lawyer: (rise) "Yes, Your Honor." (Cross-examine plaintiff's witness.)

Judge: "Plaintiff, do you have any further witnesses?"

Plaintiff's lawyer: (Rise and tell the judge yes or no, depending on whether there are more witnesses.)

Judge: (If the lawyer says "Yes," say "Call the next witness." If the lawyer says "No," ask if the defendant's case is ready.)

MOTION TO DISMISS

Defendant's lawyer: "Your Honor, I move the Court to dismiss this case, on the ground that plaintiffs have not proved their case."

Judge: (Sustain or deny the motion. If you sustain, the case is over. If you deny, the case goes on and you should say: "Denied. Proceed with the case.")

EXAMINATION OF DEFENDANT'S WITNESSES

Judge: "Does the defendant wish to call any witnesses?"

Defendant's lawyer: (rise) "Yes, Your Honor, ____

_____

(name of first witness)

Clerk: (Swear in the witness.)

Defendant's lawyer: (Begin direct examination of witness.)

 CLOSING ARGUMENTS

Judge: "_____, do you have a closing statement?"

Plaintiff's lawyer: (rise) "Yes, Your Honor."
(Make your closing statement. Sit down.)

Judge: "_____, do you have a closing statement?"

Defendant's lawyer: (rise) "Yes, Your Honor."
(Make your closing statement. Sit down.)

JUDGE'S INSTRUCTIONS TO JURY

Judge: "Members of the jury, I will now instruct you on the law in this case. Remember that you are sworn to decide this case fairly. Sympathy or prejudice must not influence your decision.
It is your duty to decide on the facts.

It is the duty of every driver of a vehicle to use at all times ordinary care for safety and to avoid collisions. When I use the words 'ordinary care,' I mean the care a reasonably careful person would use. The law does not say how a reasonably careful person would act under the circumstances of this case. That is for you to decide.

It was the duty of the plaintiff, as well as the defendant, to use ordinary care for her safety, both before and at the time of the accident.

If you decide, based on the evidence:

First, that the defendant, Charlotte Dinkins, did not come to a full stop at the red light and did not look carefully for other cars, and

Second, that the defendant, Charlotte Dinkins, was negligent in her operation of her car, and

Third, that as direct result of the defendant's negligence, the plaintiff, Didi Richards, suffered damages.

You must find for the plaintiff, unless you believe that the plaintiff is not entitled to recover for her damages because:

> First, the plaintiff's conduct was also negligent, and

> Second, the plaintiff's negligence contributed to the damages she suffered.

If you find that the plaintiff is not entitled to recover, you must find for the defendant.

If you decide for the plaintiff, you must decide on the amount of money which will reasonably and fairly pay the plaintiff for damages which resulted from the negligence of the defendant:

> The cost of restoring the plaintiff's automobile to the condition it was before the accident.

> The value of wages lost and the cash value of wages reasonably certain to be lost in the future.

> Pain and suffering.

Whether any of these damages has been proved by the evidence is for you to decide."

Bailiff: (Lead the jury out of the courtroom.)

Note to teacher: The judge may repeat the instructions to the jury in order to make sure they understand. Negligence is the failure to use ordinary care in operating the automobile.

 READING VERDICT BY THE JURY FOREPERSON

"We the jury in the above case, find in favor of the plaintiff, and assess her damages at the sum of _____ dollars ($_____)."

or

"We, the jury in the above case, find in favor of the defendant."

JUDGMENT BY THE COURT (JUDGE)

[Title of court and name of case]

This action came on for trial before the court and a jury, Honorable _____, Judge, presiding, and the issues having been duly tried and the jury having duly rendered its verdict,

It is ordered and adjudged

[that the plaintiff _____ recover of the defendant _____ the sum of _____, with interest thereon at the rate of _____ percent as provided by law, and her costs of action.]

or

[that the plaintiff take nothing, that the action be dismissed on the merits, and that the defendant _____ recover of the plaintiff _____ her costs of the action.]

Dated at _____, _____, this _____ day of _____, 19__.

Note to teacher for Lesson 23, Steps from Arrest to Criminal Trial:

Although we think the information in this lesson is important for students to know, we also feel it is important to present the facts in a way that requires more involvement than reading. Here is an idea you might try.

After the class has read through the steps once, explain the idea of turning this information into a "silent movie." Some students will be needed to be narrators for each scene (step). Other students will be needed to be the actors for each scene. Different groups of actors should act out the different scenes or steps. The group of actors should be given some time to decide how they will act out their scene without using any words. The actors will act out their scene as the narrators read the information. The class might want to put on this mini-production for another class.

FROM ARREST TO CRIMINAL TRIAL

Objective: **Students will be able to explain pre-trial procedure in the criminal cases.**

To prepare for putting on a mock criminal trial, learn what happens to a defendant from the time of the arrest to the time of the trial.

1. **Arrest:** The police take the suspect into custody to hold him/her on a criminal charge.

2. **Booking:** At the police station, a formal record of the arrest and the crime for which the accused is charged is made.

3. **First Appearance:** The accused person is taken before a judge. The judge explains what the charge against the accused is and advises the accused of his/her Constitutional rights. If the accused cannot afford a lawyer, the judge appoints one.

The judge also has to decide whether to let the accused out on BAIL, keep him/her in jail, or release him/her on a promise that he/she will appear in court for trial. (Releasing the accused on his/her promise to appear is called release on personal recognizance.)

If the accused is charged with a misdemeanor crime, he/she will also plead guilty, not guilty, or nolo contendere ("no contest," which means he/she does not admit committing the crime but agrees to be convicted and sentenced without "contesting" the charge by taking the case to trial.)

4. **Preliminary Hearing:** The prosecuting attorney presents evidence to convince the judge there is reason to go on with the case (that there is "probable cause"—reasonable cause—to believe the accused committed a crime.) The accused is released if the judge decides there is no probable cause.

5. **Grand Jury Indictment on Information:** In most states, when the prosecuting attorney has enough facts from the police and witnesses, he/she files a legal paper called an INFORMATION at the court. The information states the charges for which the accused will stand trial. This method is used for almost all misdemeanor cases (less serious crimes), but for felony cases some states may use a GRAND JURY instead.

A grand jury is made up of registered voters (23 in most states) who are picked at random. The grand jury holds a hearing at which the prosecutor must present evidence against the accused. If the grand jury finds that there is enough evidence for the case to go ahead, they will issue an INDICTMENT. The indictment (sometimes called a "true bill") states the charges for which the accused will stand trial. If the grand jury finds there is not enough evidence, they will issue a "no bill," and the case will go no further.

GRAND JURY
SUBPOENA

To ..... *Beatrice Backlimp* ..... ,Greetings:
    You are hereby commanded, all excuses and delays set aside, that you be and appear in the Grand Jury Room on ..... *September 22, 1980* ..... , then and there to give evidence before the Grand Jury, and in this no wise omit, under legal penalty.

Note to teacher: At a grand jury hearing, only the evidence against the accused is presented. In many states the person under investigation is permitted to be accompanied by counsel, but counsel cannot communicate with anyone except the client. Although the person under investigation cannot present evidence, he/she can, of course, refuse to testify under the 5th Amendment.

6. **The Arraignment:** The accused person appears before the judge in order to enter a plea on the case. The accused can plead guilty, not guilty, or nolo contendere. If the accused pleads not guilty, he/she can choose whether he/she wants to be tried by a judge or by a jury.

7. **Plea Bargaining:** The prosecuting attorney and the defense lawyer try to reach an agreement. If the defendant (the accused) agrees to plead guilty, the prosecutor may agree to let the defendant plead guilty to a less serious crime than the one with which he/she is charged.

8. **The Trial:** (See pages 94–98 to review STEPS in a trial.)

Note to teacher: If at all possible, try to take the class to the court building to see where some of these procedures take place. Call either the clerk of the court or the prosecuting attorney's office to help set up the field trip.

Objective: Students will participate in putting on their own mock criminal trial.

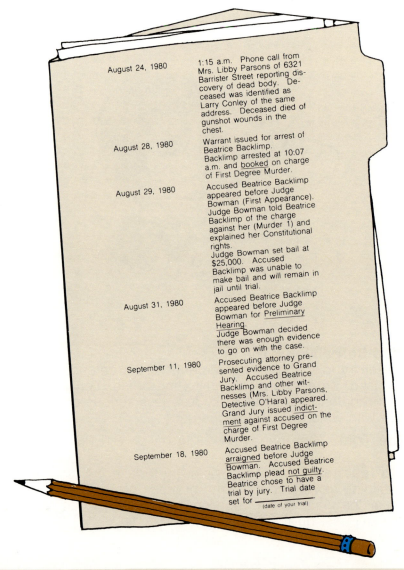

August 24, 1980	1:15 a.m. Phone call from Mrs. Libby Parsons of 6321 Barrister Street reporting discovery of dead body. Deceased was identified as Larry Conley of the same address. Deceased died of gunshot wounds in the chest.
August 28, 1980	Warrant issued for arrest of Beatrice Backlimp. Backlimp arrested at 10:07 a.m. and booked on charge of First Degree Murder.
August 29, 1980	Accused Beatrice Backlimp appeared before Judge Bowman (First Appearance). Judge Bowman told Beatrice Backlimp of the charge against her (Murder 1) and explained her Constitutional rights. Judge Bowman set bail at $25,000. Accused Backlimp was unable to make bail and will remain in jail until trial.
August 31, 1980	Accused Beatrice Backlimp appeared before Judge Bowman for Preliminary Hearing. Judge Bowman decided there was enough evidence to go on with the case.
September 11, 1980	Prosecuting attorney presented evidence to Grand Jury. Accused Beatrice Backlimp and other witnesses (Mrs. Libby Parsons, Detective O'Hara) appeared. Grand Jury issued indictment against accused on the charge of First Degree Murder.
September 18, 1980	Accused Beatrice Backlimp arraigned before Judge Bowman. Accused Beatrice Backlimp plead not guilty. Beatrice chose to have a trial by jury. Trial date set for _____ (date of your trial)

Note to teacher: Whether or not the police had enough evidence to obtain an arrest warrant for Beatrice is not raised in this lesson. This lesson focuses on post-arrest legal procedures. It might be a good idea to ask a lawyer or police officer to appear as a resource person to help discuss some of these steps in the pre-trial procedure.

1. One Judge
2. Two Prosecuting Attorneys
3. Two Defense Attorneys
4. One Court Reporter
5. One Bailiff
6. One Clerk
7. Jury Members
8. Defendant—Beatrice Backlimp
9. Witnesses:
   Mrs. Parsons, Landlady
   Detective O'Hara, Police Investigator
   Reverend Brooks
   Sheryl Harper, Friend at party
   Elizabeth Franklin

Students should work together in groups specified below to prepare for the trial. The students should understand the information and follow the directions given on their work group sheets.

COURT PROCEDURE FOR A

MOCK CRIMINAL TRIAL

Note to teacher: In actual trials the witnesses are generally kept outside the courtroom until they are called to the stand so that they don't hear the testimony of the other witnesses. You may decide whether or not you wish to follow this procedure.

 OPENING OF THE COURT

(The bailiff rises and says in a loud, clear voice:)

Bailiff: "All rise. The Court of _____ is now open and in session, the Honorable Judge _____ presiding." (Judge enters. Everyone rises and remains standing until the judge sits down.)

Bailiff: "All persons having business before the court may now approach the bench."

Judge: "The case of the State versus _____. Is the prosecution ready?"

Prosecuting Attorney: "The prosecution is ready."

Judge: "Is the defendant ready?"

Defense Attorney: "The defendant is ready."

 JURY SELECTION

Clerk: (Swears in all jury members at one time.) "The jury will rise, raise your right hands and be sworn in."

"Do you solemnly swear that you will well and truly try the issues now to be given to you; that you will speak nothing to anyone of the business or matters you have in hand, nor will you let anyone speak to you about the same but in court and when you are agreed upon any verdict, you will keep it secret until you deliver it up in court? Do you all swear?"

Jury: "I do."

Clerk: "You may be seated."

OPENING STATEMENTS

Judge: "Does the prosecution have an opening statement?"

Prosecuting Attorney: (Rise) "Yes, Your Honor." (Make opening statement, sit down.)

Judge: "_____ do you have
(defense attorney)
any opening statement?"

Defense Attorney: "Yes your honor." (Rise and make opening statement)

 EXAMINATION OF PROSECUTION WITNESSES

Judge: "Will the prosecution call its first witness?"

Prosecuting Attorney: (Rise) _____
(name of first witness)

Clerk: "First Witness, _____ shall take the stand." (The clerk should swear in each witness.)

Prosecuting Attorney: (Begin direct examination of witness)

Judge: "Does the defense wish to cross-examine this witness?"

Defense Attorney: "Yes, Your Honor." (Cross-examine prosecution witness.)

Judge: "Does the prosecution have any further witnesses?"

Prosecuting Attorney: (Rise and tell the judge "yes" or "no", depending on whether you have more witnesses.)

Judge: (If prosecuting attorney says "yes" say "Call the next witness," if the lawyer says "no," ask if the defense is ready.)

 MOTION TO DISMISS

Defense Attorney: "Your Honor, I move the court to dismiss this case on the ground that the prosecution has not proved the defendant guilty of any crime."

118

Judge: (Sustain or deny the motion. If you sustain, the case is over. If you deny, the case goes on and you should say: "Denied, proceed with the case.")

 EXAMINATION OF DEFENSE WITNESSES

Judge: "Does the defense wish to call any witnesses?"

Defense Attorney: (Rise) "Yes, Your Honor, _____ (name of first witness) (Begin direct examination of witness.)

Judge: "Does the prosecution wish to cross-examine this witness?"

Prosecuting Attorney: (Rise) "Yes, Your Honor." (cross-examine defense witness)

Judge: "Does the defense have any further witnesses?"

Defense Attorney: (Rise and tell the judge "yes" or "no" depending on whether you have more witnesses.)

Judge: (If defense lawyer says "yes" ask for the next witness to be called. If the lawyer says "no," say) "We will have a one minute recess so the lawyers can prepare their closing statements." (after one minute, say): "Court come to order."

 CLOSING STATEMENTS

Judge: "Does the prosecution have a closing statement?"

Prosecuting Attorney: (Rise) Yes, Your Honor." (Make your closing statement)

Judge: "Does the defense have a closing statement?"

Defense Attorney: (Rise) "Yes, Your Honor." (Make your closing statement)

 JUDGE'S INSTRUCTIONS TO JURY

Judge: Members of the jury, I will now instruct you on the law in this case. Remember that you are sworn to decide this case fairly. Sympathy or prejudice must not influence your decision.

It is your duty to decide on the facts. A criminal defendant is thought to be innocent until proven guilty. If any one of you have a reasonable doubt about the defendant's guilt, the defendant has not been proven guilty.

The defendant is charged with first degree murder. You may find her guilty of first degree or second degree murder.

To find her guilty of second degree murder, you must decide that the following statements are true.

First, that Larry Conley died on or about September 2nd, 1980, in the city of _____, state of _____ as a result of the defendant shooting him in the chest.

Second, that the defendant intended to kill Larry Conley or she knew that her act of shooting him would probably result in his death.

To find her guilty of first degree murder, you must also decide based on the evidence:

That the defendant planned to kill Larry Conley and thought about the matter cooly and fully before she shot him.

If you find the defendant guilty, you must state in your verdict whether she is guilty of first degree or second degree murder. However, if based on the evidence you heard, you have a reasonable doubt that the first and second statements are true, then you must decide that the defendant is not guilty of murder.

Bailiff: (Lead the jury out of the courtroom.)

Note to teacher: The judge may repeat the instructions if the jurors have trouble understanding them. A reasonable doubt is "a fair and honest doubt growing out of the evidence or lack of evidence." It is "a state of mind which would cause a person to hesitate in making a decision in his/her own life."

 JURY VERDICT

Jury: (Return to courtroom and sit down)

Judge: "Has the jury reached a verdict?"

Jury Foreperson: (Rise) "Yes, Your Honor. We the jury in the case of The State versus Beatrice Backlimp in the court of _____ find the defendant, Beatrice Backlimp,

(guilty as charged

or

guilty of second degree murder

or

not guilty of the offense charged).

 JUDGMENT

_____
(name of Court)

_____
(name of Case)

This action came on for trial before the court and a jury, Honorable _____ Judge, presiding, and the issues having been duly tried and the jury having duly rendered its verdict—

(Verdict against Defendant)

It is ordered and adjudged that the defendant has been convicted upon her plea of (guilty or not guilty) of the offense of _____ charged; and the court having asked the defendant whether she has anything to say why judgment should not be pronounced and no sufficient cause to the contrary being shown or appearing to the court,

It is adjudged that the defendant is guilty as charged and convicted.

It is ordered and adjudged by the court that defendant be imprisoned in the penitentiary of this state for the term of _____ years, and she pay the costs of this prosecution, taxed at _____ dollars, and that she stand committed to the custody of the sheriff until she be legally discharged.

(Verdict for Defendant)

It is, therefore, considered by the court that said defendant go hence without delay, fully acquitted and discharged.

JUSTICE

Objective: **Students will analyze what they learned from taking part in a mock trial.**

Students will discuss the responsibilities of every person to work for justice in our society.

your mock trial

DEBRIEFING

1. What do you think was the most important thing you learned from putting on your trial?

2. "Juries have an important role, but often don't feel as important as they should." Do you agree or disagree with this statement? Explain your reasons.

3. Can you give any reasons why a trial might take months to prepare?

4. Did you see any reasons why it might be necessary to have a lawyer when going to court?

5. What part did you play in the trial? What did you learn about trials from the part you played?

6. Your class probably can't do the trial over again, but if you could, what would you do differently?

7. Is there other evidence that would have been useful for the lawyers to present? What would it have been and how would it have been useful?

8. Are there other witnesses you would have called? Why would they have been helpful to prove that side of the case?

9. What other question (questions) would you have asked the witnesses who testified?

10. What part did you play in the trial? Explain how you felt playing this part.

11. Important elements in whether or not a trial is fair are:
    —was the jury unbiased?
    —did the defendant have the opportunity to have a lawyer?
    —was unreliable evidence excluded from the trial?
    —was a transcript made of the trial?
    —were witnesses presented and cross-examined?
    —was the defendant present in the courtroom?
    —did the judge keep order in the courtroom and apply the law correctly?
    Based on these points, do you think the defendant in your trial received a fair trial? Explain your answer.

Note to teacher: Most of the questions focus on the students analyzing their trial. You might want to add other questions concerning the "legality" of what happened in the trial. Such questions as "Did the jury really have enough evidence to reach a verdict?" might be asked. Also included is a question which focuses on the students' personal experience in participating in the trial. We feel that a strength of a mock trial as a teaching method is that it allows students to gain understanding of the feelings of participants in a real trial and gives them experience in identifying and articulating their own feelings.

12. Take a stand on the opinion line.

Some people believe that people will always be treated unfairly by others and that justice for all is impossible.

Other people think that justice for all is possible when many people who want justice for all will work to have it.

If you agree with these people stand all the way to the left of the line.

If you agree with these people stand all the way to the right of the line.

If your opinion is somewhere in the middle of these two opinions stand at the spot on the line that best represents what you think about this question.

Note to teacher: Draw the "opinion line" across the front of the blackboard, and place the extreme positions given on this page at either end of the line. Ask a few students to come and take a stand at the spot on the line that best represents their opinion on this question. Ask them why they are standing where they are and what reasons they have to support their opinion.

See page 84 for another description of an opinion line and ways to use it in the classroom.

Objective: **Students will be able to define words introduced in Section III.**

Match the words listed below with the correct definition. Look in the glossary to check your work. Write the definition for any word you missed.

a. bail

b. indictment

c. book

d. grand jury

e. sentence

f. plea bargaining

g. verdict

h. deposition

i. arraignment

j. damages

k. negligence

_i_ 1. The accused person comes before a judge and pleads guilty, not guilty, or nolo contendere.

_a_ 2. Money the judge orders the accused to pay to the court to make certain the accused will appear for the trial.

_j_ 3. Money the court orders to be paid to the person who has suffered a loss in a civil case.

_h_ 4. Testimony of a witness under oath taken before a trial.

_d_ 5. A group of citizens who hear accusations of a crime and decide if there is enough evidence against the accused to proceed with a criminal trial.

_b_ 6. A formal accusation made by a grand jury.

_f_ 7. Attempts at making a deal between the prosecutor and the defense lawyer that the defendant will plead guilty to and the prosecutor will charge him with a less serious crime or that the prosecutor will recommend a lighter sentence.

_k_ 8. The failure of a person to use care in a situation that causes harm to someone or something.

_g_ 9. The decision made by a jury at a trial.

_e_ 10. A punishment or penalty.

_c_ 11. Make a formal police record of an arrest.

NEWSBULLETIN REVIEW—SECTION III

Objective: **Students will be able to answer questions on a class test about information presented in Section III.**

Note to students: This lesson is a review quiz. You can use it to check how much you have learned so far about courts and trials. Some classes have turned these reviews into newsbulletins. When your answers get printed in a newsbulletin, they help other people learn what you have learned.

Note to teacher: Have the students turn to the blank newsbulletin on the next page. The class may vote on the name or letterhead of the newsbulletin. Then, each student should complete every section of the newsbulletin by answering the questions or giving his/her opinion.

The newsbulletin technique can be used as the evaluation measure or test. The "best" articles can be printed on ditto masters and made to look like a real newspaper. The newsbulletin should stimulate the students to try hard to answer all the questions on the "test."

NEWSBULLETIN

EDITORIAL

Are jury trials a fair way of deciding a serious criminal case? Give reasons to support your answer.

NEWS PICTURE

Draw a picture of the most important thing you learned by participating in a mock trial.

TRUE/FALSE

1. In a civil case, the defendant makes the complaint against the plaintiff. _False_

2. If a person can't pay the amount of bail set by the judge, the judge must lower the bail to a lesser amount of money. _False_

3. The bailiff is responsible for the jury during a trial. _True_

4. Witnesses can't say anything to the lawyers until the day of the trial. _False_

5. During a trial, a jury member has a duty to decide which facts are true and which witnesses and evidence to believe. _True_

6. Negligence means being careless in certain circumstances. _True_

glossary

ACQUIT	Find not guilty.
AFFIRM	Approve the decision of the lower court in a case.
APPEAL	Take a case to a higher court for review.
ARRAIGNMENT	Bringing the accused before a judge to hear the complaint so the accused may enter a plea of guilty or not guilty.
ATTORNEY	Lawyer, counsel.
BAIL	Money that the judge makes the accused person leave with the court in order to be released before trial. If the accused fails to appear for trial he/she forfeits the bail money.
BAILIFF	An officer of the court who has charge of the accused person while he or she is in the courtroom, and also looks after the jurors.
BOOK	Enter an arrested person's name and charge in police records.
CIVIL CASE	An action in which one person sues another person for damages or other relief because of some injury or wrong done.
CLERK	Court official who keeps court records, official files.
COMPLAINT	The first paper filed in a civil lawsuit which states the wrong done to the plaintiff by the defendant and a request for a remedy by the court.
CONFLICT	A disagreement, usually between two or more persons.
CONTRACT	An agreement between two or more persons in which one makes a promise in exchange for something of value.

CONTRIBUTORY NEGLIGENCE	Negligence on the part of the plaintiff which helped cause his/her injury or damages.
COURT	Place where civil and criminal trials are held.
COURT REPORTER	A legal stenographer who records court proceedings.
CRIMINAL CASE	An action brought by the state, county, or city against an individual, charging the person with committing a crime.
DAMAGES	Money that a court, in a civil case, orders paid to a person (usually the plaintiff) who has suffered loss by another person who caused the loss (usually the defendant).
DEFENSE ATTORNEY	The lawyer who represents the defendant.
DEPOSITION	Testimony (statement) of a witness, under oath, taken before the trial in answer to questions by lawyers for both sides.
DUE PROCESS	Procedures to protect individual rights in legal proceedings.
EVICT	Put a person out of a dwelling for failure to meet a legal obligation; for example, for failure to pay rent.
EVIDENCE	Proof; witnesses' statements or physical objects presented at a trial to prove something is true or happened.
EXAMINATION	The questioning of a witness by a lawyer at a trial or deposition. When the lawyer who called the witness to the stand questions the witness, the examination is *direct*. When the opposing lawyer is questioning, it is *cross examination*.
FACT	Something that really exists, a known event or thing.
FELONY	A very serious crime such as murder or armed robbery, where imprisonment is usually for more than one year.
GRAND JURY	A jury which hears complaints and accusations of a crime, decides whether there are sufficient facts to support the charges, and can make formal accusations or indictments.

HEARSAY	Evidence that a witness has heard from someone else.
IMPARTIAL	Fair, without prejudice, unbiased.
INDICTMENT	A formal accusation of a crime made against a person by a grand jury upon the request of the prosecutor.
INFORMATION	The paper filed by the prosecutor formally stating the charges against the accused.
INITIAL APPEARANCE	The bringing of the accused before the judge for explanation of charges against the accused and of his/her constitutional rights. At this time the judge decides whether to release the accused on bail.
INTERPRET	To make clear the meaning.
JUDGE	A person appointed or elected to hear and decide cases, and to make certain that legal procedures are followed.
JUDGMENT	An order by a judge on a case; decision.
JURISDICTION	The area and types of cases which a court has authority to hear and decide.
JURY	A group of people (usually twelve), chosen by law and found satisfactory to both sides in a lawsuit, to decide the facts of the case. and enter a verdict.
LAWYER	A person who has been licensed to represent others in legal matters.
LIABILITY	A legal responsibility, obligation, or debt.
MALICE	An intent to do a wrongful act and to do injury; evil intent.
MANSLAUGHTER	The unlawful killing of another without malice. Manslaughter may be either voluntary or involuntary.
MISDEMEANOR	A less serious crime, such as resisting arrest or petty larceny, where the imprisonment cannot be for more than one year.
MOCK	Make-believe, pretend.
MURDER	The unlawful killing of another person that is planned in advance with evil intent (malice).
NEGLIGENCE	The failure of a person to use reasonable care to avoid injury to others.

NEGOTIATE	To discuss or confer in order to resolve a problem.
OVERRULE	To rule that a decision by a lower court is invalid; reverse.
PARTY	The person who brings a lawsuit against someone or the person against whom a lawsuit is brought.
PERJURY	Lying while under oath.
PETIT (PETTY) JURY	A trial jury which decides questions of fact in a court case.
PETITION	A formal request to the court asking for some remedy for a harm done.
PLAINTIFF	The person or party who files a complaint and brings a legal action against another person or party.
PLEA BARGAINING	A discussion in which the prosecutor and the defense attorney try to reach an agreement that the defendant will plead guilty and the prosecutor will charge the defendant with a less serious crime.
PRECEDENT	Previous court decisions used for guidance in deciding questions of law in a similar case.
PREDICT	Forecast or tell beforehand.
PROCEDURE	The rules courts have for handling lawsuits in court. Rules of procedure control such things as testimony and questioning witnesses.
PROSECUTING ATTORNEY	Lawyer who defends the interest and rights of the people of the state against the defendant in a criminal trial.
PROVE	Show with evidence that something exists or is true.
RESOLVE	Settle or solve a problem.
SENTENCE	The punishment or penalty given by the judge to a person who has pleaded guilty to a crime or who has been found guilty by a jury.
SUBPOENA	A court order requiring a person to appear in court to give testimony.
TESTIFY	To give evidence under oath.

TESTIMONY	Evidence given by a witness under oath.
TORT	A wrong or injury done to a person for which the wronged person can bring a civil suit.
TRANSCRIPT	The record of a court proceeding.
TRIAL	A proceeding in a court for the purpose of settling a legal problem by considering the evidence on both sides.
VERDICT	The decision made by the jury in a trial.
VOIR DIRE	The questioning of possible jurors by the judge and the lawyers to decide whether they are able to decide the case in a fair and impartial manner.
WARRANT OF ARREST	A written order to arrest a certain person issued by a court to a peace officer (police officer, sheriff, etc.).
WITNESS	A person who has knowledge of facts having to do with a case being tried and who gives testimony.
WRIT OF HABEAS CORPUS	A legal document used to find out if a person is being detained or imprisoned unlawfully. It literally means "You have the body," and orders the prison official who has the person in custody to release the person for a hearing. This writ is often used by persons in prison when appealing their case to the Supreme Court.

Note to teacher:

A lawyer or law-student could be very helpful in preparing for the trial and/or viewing the trial and discussing what happened in the debriefing session.

In order to make the most effective use of the special expertise of the lawyer or law student in putting on a mock trial, it may be helpful to provide the resource person with general guidelines concerning his/her participation. The participation of the law resource person can be as extensive as his/her schedule permits: some may be available only for the trial and debriefing; others may be able to participate in several days of pretrial preparation in addition to the trial and debriefing. Following are some suggested guidelines for lawyers and law students assisting with mock trials:

Debriefing

The law professional can provide students with a tremendous pride of accomplishment by offering praise to the participants; because of the law professional's particular credibility in this setting, such praise is special and should not be overlooked. Similarly, the law professional should be especially sensitive in giving criticism to phrase comments in a constructive, encouraging way.

1. The law professional can provide students with a sense of reality by offering comments and anecdotes about what happens in a real trial and how the mock trial compares to a real trial. The ability of the students to relate to the trial process is enhanced by explanations which are based on personal experiences of the law professional rather than on bare "book" explanations.

2. The law professional can provide students a meaningful critique of the mock trial by demonstrating procedural mistakes and responding to questions which arise about the steps in the procedure, about the appeal process, about the differences between civil and criminal trials, etc.

Preparation

1. The law professional can provide students encouragement and guidance in preparing for trial, but should avoid doing the work for the students; the law professional is in the classroom as a special type of teacher, not to be the lawyer and write the best questions, etc. This may be difficult for persons who have not had prior experience in a teaching capacity. In helping the student lawyers to draft arguments and questions for trial, the law professional can give examples as starting points for the students or ask students what they think.

2. In order to maximize the involvement of the law professional the teacher should have the students do preliminary work on trial preparation prior to the appearance of the law professional. If the students have some work to show the law professional, the temptation to do the work for the students can be more easily avoided and the law professional will have a better indication of the level of work and needs of the students. Because the law professional may inadvertently devote time in an unbalanced fashion to one team or another, it is often wise for the teacher to suggest time limits for the law professional's involvement with each side; this may be done on an alternating basis (i. e., 5 minutes with team A, 5 minutes with team B, 5 minutes with team A, etc.).

    Some time should also be allocated to the student judge. The law professional can make sure the judge understands how to respond to objections during the trial.

INFORMATION FOR WITNESSES

Your job is to answer questions truthfully about the facts of the case.

Read the case summary and your character's deposition testimony carefully so that you really know what happened.

Try to imagine what other facts might go along with the facts provided. For example, think about what else your character might have seen or heard at the time of the accident or crime, what he/she might have felt when it happened, and what his/her car, job, driving record, or police records, and the rest of his/her life might be like. Be prepared for the lawyers to ask questions about some of these things before the trial and at the trial.

You may make up facts if you are asked a question about something not included in the facts provided.

Your answers can add to the facts given but should not change the story given in your deposition statement. Your deposition statement was made by you under oath before the trial.

When you testify at the trial, you should not read your deposition statement. You are supposed to know what happened. The lawyer for the other side may look at your deposition to make sure you are not changing your story.

MOCK CIVIL TRIAL

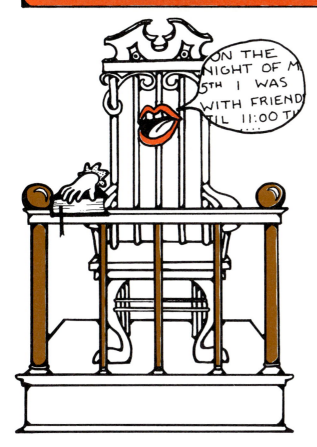

Witness

The lawyers for Mrs. Richards and Mrs. Dinkins took depositions of the witnesses in this case. Following are statements made under oath by the witnesses.

Doctor Perkins: "My name is Dr. Perkins. I have been a medical doctor for 25 years. I was on duty in the emergency room the night of January 2, 1980. Officer MacArthur brought in Mrs. Didi Richards. We x-rayed her wrist and found a hairline fracture. It is not a very serious break. We put a small cast on her wrist. I told her that it would take about 6 weeks to heal and that it would be weak for some time after that. I told her to come back if it gave her any pain. I saw her 8 weeks later when I took off her cast. I didn't see her again until today."

Officer MacArthur: "My name is Officer John MacArthur. I have been a patrol officer for ten years. I was cruising down Lindell and saw two cars rammed into each other. The drivers of the cars were women. One woman, Mrs. Dinkins, was standing near Mrs. Richards' car door when I approached. Mrs. Richards seemed to be in pain. She said that she felt terrible and that she thought her wrist was broken. Mrs. Dinkins appeared unhurt. When I questioned them about the accident, both women claimed that it was not their fault. I found a passerby, Mr. Henry Oliver. He said that he saw the whole thing. Mr. Oliver told me that he didn't see the Volkswagen slow down as it approached the intersection. However, the night of the accident I had noticed that Mr. Oliver's breath smelled of liquor. I then took Mrs. Richards to the hospital."

MORE STATEMENTS

Didi Richards: "I am 27 years old. I have been working as a cocktail waitress at the Golf Lounge for two years. I am divorced and I have a four year old child.

"I am in the habit of taking the same route home from work every night. I go through the intersection where the accident happened very often. On the night of the accident I left work at 11:15 p.m. I was anxious to get home as early as I could because my child was sick.

"As I approached the intersection of Lindell and Taylor Streets, the light was flashing yellow. I slowed down, looked around, saw no cars and started through the intersection. Midway through the intersection I heard brakes screech and saw a car coming at me. Then, wham!! Mrs. Dinkins' car hit me broadside.

"I am a very careful driver. If Mrs. Dinkins had stopped at the red stop light like she was supposed to, I know the accident could have been avoided.

"I was thrown across the seat by the crash. I broke my wrist and was bruised all over my arms and legs from the accident. I have a nervous condition also. I was tense and nervous for weeks after the accident. I haven't been able to carry trays of drinks at the lounge since the accident. My legs are still a horrible sight! The accident was Mrs. Dinkins' fault. I have suffered a great deal because of her carelessness."

Charlotte Dinkins: "I am 57 years old. I have worked as a registered nurse at Belnor Hospital for 15 years. On the night of January 2, 1980 I was driving my Chevy Nova home, going north on Taylor. I was tired from a long day at work.

"There was a flashing red light at the intersection of Lindell and Taylor. I made a stop and then continued into the intersection. Before I knew it, a car sped into my path. I applied the brakes, but couldn't avoid hitting the car. I was shaken up by the accident, but was not hurt. The lady who was driving the car was crying. She said that the crash was all my fault. I think it was her fault."

Henry Oliver: "I am Henry Oliver. I am 62 years old and live at 241 Taylor Avenue. On the night of January 2, 1980, I had spent a few hours with some friends in a neighborhood bar. I was walking home on the sidewalk on Lindell when the accident happened. It looked to me that the Volkswagen did not slow down as it approached the intersection. Both drivers seemed to spot each other at the same time and applied their brakes. The cars collided. I didn't get a good look at the Chevy Nova until after the crash. I admit I had been drinking that night. I still knew what I was doing."

MOCK CRIMINAL TRIAL

Witness

STATEMENTS

LANDLADY: "My name is Libby Parsons. Ever since my husband passed away I have managed the apartment house at 6321 Barrister Street by myself. Larry Conley rented the apartment upstairs from my apartment since April. He seemed to be a nice man and had a good job working with computers. He always paid his rent on time. He often had friends over but he was generally pretty quiet."

"On Friday, August 24, 1980, around 1:00 a.m. I heard a loud noise, sort of like a firecracker, come from upstairs. I went upstairs to find out what was going on. It took me a few minutes to get dressed, but when I went I saw Beatrice Backlimp go past me and run down the street. I didn't know her name, but I recognized her because she had visited Larry's apartment before.

"Larry's door was open. I called Larry's name but there was no answer. I looked into the apartment from the doorway. I walked in a little way and looked around. Then, I saw Larry's head and shoulders on the floor visible from behind the sofa. I went to him and saw that he had been shot. I ran downstairs and called the police."

POLICE INVESTIGATOR: "My name is Dective O'Hara. I have been an investigator for the Police Department for 6 years. I was called to 6321 Barrister to investigate a homicide. I arrived at the scene of the crime about 3 a.m. I judged the deceased, Larry Conley, to be dead about 2 hours. He had been shot in the chest with a .32 automatic pistol. Mrs. Parsons, the landlady, told me she saw Beatrice Backlimp, wearing a green coat, running from the apartment at 1:45 a.m. Later, I found out that Beatrice's father, Henry Backlimp, had a .32 caliber pistol registered in his name."

FRIEND AT PARTY: "My name is Sheryl Harper. I attended the party at 5330 Hip Street on August 24, 1980. I was shocked to see Larry Conley there with another girl, Beatrice Backlimp, because I thought he and Elizabeth Franklin were really tight. I knew Elizabeth was crazy about Larry. She even told me they might be getting married some day. I never saw Beatrice Backlimp before the party. She was a stranger to everyone. I called Elizabeth to tell her about Larry and Beatrice because I thought it was my duty as her friend. Elizabeth and Larry both had bad tempers and they often had fights."

MORE STATEMENTS

BEATRICE BACKLIMP (DEFEN-DANT): "My name is Beatrice Backlimp. I quit school two years ago. I'm nineteen and work at the Burger Chef downtown. About August 15th I met Larry for the first time. I had seen him often when he came in to buy lunch and thought he was handsome. He told me he had another girl friend who was real jealous, but we kept seeing each other everyday for lunch. Then, he invited me to a party on Friday, August 24, 1980. He said he had broken up with his old girl friend and he wanted to start going with me. We were having a wonderful time dancing at the party when Larry looked straight at me and called me Elizabeth. Then Larry wouldn't even tell me who Elizabeth was so I became furious and demanded that he take me right home.

"I couldn't sleep and started to feel bad at losing my temper at Larry. When I got over to his house to apologize I found his door open but he wasn't there. I called up Sue Robbins but she had not seen him since he left the party. Then I was upset and worried and ran out of Larry's apartment. I was mad at Larry but not enough to kill him."

ELIZABETH FRANKLIN: "My name is Elizabeth Franklin. I am 18 years old and attend Central High School. My parents want me to go to Junior College next year but I want to get married. I don't like school too much but I do like boys.

"On Friday, August 24, 1980, there was a big party on Hip Street. My boy friend, Larry Conley, invited me to go with him but my mother refused to let me go because I had promised to babysit that night. Larry and I were really tight and I was depressed that I could not go to the party. Larry said I was the only girl for him and that he wouldn't even go the party without me.

"Later that night a friend called me from the party and told me Larry was there dancing with Beatrice Backlimp. I was furious and rushed over to his house. Larry and I both have a bad temper and when he came home we had a big fight."

REVEREND BROOKS (CHARAC-TER WITNESS): "My name is Reverend Brooks. I have known Beatrice and her family ever since Beatrice was a little girl. She attended Church and Sunday School regularly. Beatrice worked hard in school. Her parents were always proud of her. I don't believe she could ever kill anyone."

SPECIAL INFORMATION FOR PLAINTIFF'S LAWYERS AND PROSECUTING ATTORNEYS

In a CIVIL CASE your job is to convince the jury to believe the plaintiff's story and give the plaintiff what he/she wants.

In a CRIMINAL CASE your job is to convince the jury to believe beyond a reasonable doubt that the defendant is guilty.

The first thing to do is to about the case.

In a CIVIL CASE the major points for you to prove are:

1. Something happened, <u>and</u>
2. the defendant caused it, <u>and</u>
3. the plaintiff or the plaintiff's property was hurt in some way because of what happened.

In a CRIMINAL CASE the major points for you to prove are:

1. A crime occurred, <u>and</u>
2. the defendant had the opportunity and the motive to do it and did it.

Make an outline of the story you want to prove. What FACTS prove a major point in your story?

In a CIVIL CASE:

1. What facts show that something happened?
2. What facts show that the defendant caused it?
3. What facts show that the plaintiff or the plaintiff's property was hurt as a result?

In a CRIMINAL CASE:

1. What facts show that a crime occurred?
2. What facts show that the defendant had the opportunity and motive and did do it?

After you have made a list of the facts, follow the GENERAL INFORMATION FOR LAWYERS on pages 141–143.

SPECIAL INFORMATION FOR DEFENDANT'S LAWYERS

In a CIVIL CASE your job is to convince the jury that the defendant should not be liable for what the plaintiff is demanding.

In a CRIMINAL CASE your job is to convince the jury to believe that there is a reasonable doubt about defendant's guilt.

The first thing to do is to about the case.

In a CIVIL CASE the major points for you to show are:

1. whatever happened was not the defendant's fault. (That is, the plaintiff was just as much at fault) *or*

2. the plaintiff had no injuries or damages as a result.

In a CRIMINAL CASE the major point for you to make is:

the defendant is innocent. (The defendant had no motive and no opportunity and did not do it.)

Make an outline of the story you want to prove. What FACTS prove a major point in your story?

In a CIVIL CASE:

1. What facts show that it was not the defendant's fault? (or that it was the plaintiff's fault?)

2. What facts show that the plaintiff had no injuries or damages as a result?

In a CRIMINAL CASE:

1. What facts show that the defendant is not guilty?

After you have completed your list of facts, follow the GENERAL INFORMATION FOR LAWYERS, pages 141–143.

GENERAL INFORMATION FOR LAWYERS

GET YOUR FACTS TOGETHER!

Getting the facts together to prove your side of the case.

To help you prove your case, you want to get all the facts together. Then you want to make certain that you bring out the facts that are most helpful to your case.

What witnesses are most helpful to your side of the case? Why are they most helpful? What physical evidence is most helpful to your case? What is the best way to present that evidence?

1. **Facts weakening the other side's story**

   To help you prove your side of the story, you will also want to show all the weaknesses in the other side:

   that their evidence is not reliable (for example, that a witness may be mistaken or not be telling the truth)

   that their evidence doesn't make sense

   that their evidence doesn't prove anything

   that there are facts which make their story less believable.

   What facts do you know which weaken the other side? Add these facts to your list.

2. **Additional facts**

   Think about whether there might be additional facts, not provided in the case summary or depositions, which might be helpful to your side. Which witnesses should you question about these possible additional facts? What physical evidence might show these facts?

3. **Talk with the witnesses** to see if there are any additional facts and to make sure the witnesses haven't changed their stories. You must convince each witness to tell you *all* the facts. It is important for you to know the facts harmful to your case whch may come out at the trial. Tell each witness that a lawyer keeps *confidential* (does not tell anyone else) any information which is private or which might weaken your side of the case. Add any additional facts to your list.

4. **Review pages—"Steps to Bring a Case to Trial"** so you know what to prepare for in the trial.

PREPARE FOR THE TRIAL

1. **Decide which witnesses to call to the stand.** You should call only witnesses who can say something in support of your side. Give a list of these witnesses and the order in which you will call them to the stand to the court clerk.

2. **Write questions.** Each lawyer should write a set of questions for the witnesses he/she will question at the trial. (Include witnesses who will be called by the other side.) Make up questions which ask for FACTS.

> For example, if one of the facts in your story is, "Before that day, the dog bit 3 people." You may ask the following questions to get that fact into the evidence:
>
> Has the dog ever bitten anyone else?
>
> How many persons has the dog bitten?

Looking at the fact list you have prepared will help you make sure that your questions ask for facts which are *relevant* to the case. Review pages 55 and 56 on the types of questions not to ask.

All witnesses you call to the stand should be asked identifying questions, such as:

What is your name?   What is your occupation?

Where do you live?   Where do you work?

Make sure that you ask only for facts favorable to your side of the story. Sometimes, this may mean that you have no questions to ask certain witnesses!

If you have *physical evidence* to present, you will need questions to ask a witness who can identify the evidence.

3. **Write opening and closing statements.** Look at the case outline prepared by your lawyer group. This should also be the outline for the opening and closing statement. (The opening statement is the story you hope to prove. The closing statement is what you think you did prove during the trial. The closing statement might have to be changed by the time you use it if there are surprises during the trial.)

4. Prepare for the voir dire (Jury Selection). Check with your teacher to see if you will have time to do this in class.
If you do a voir dire at the trial, you will question each jury candidate to decide if you want him/her on the jury.

Your aim is to choose jurors who will be fair to your side.
Here are some questions you may want to ask jury candidates.

Are you related to the accused person, to the judge, the lawyers, or do you have any personal knowledge about them?

Do you hold any prejudices against the race, creed, or color of the accused person or lawyers in this case?

Have you read any stories in the newspapers about this case? If so, could you put aside those stories and decide the case only on evidence presented in the courtroom?

Has anyone close to you been involved in a similar type of case?

Look at the facts of the case which will come out at a trial.
Is there anything about the people or events involved in the case that might cause a juror to rule against your side even if all the facts are in your favor? Write your own questions about these points.

Note to teacher: The student writing voir dire questions may need some help. Encourage the student to think through the points mentioned in the instructions and convert the points into appropriate questions.

THE TRIAL ITSELF

1. **Select the jury.** Ask each jury candidate the questions you prepared and mark the answers on the chart given to you by the bailiff. After all the questioning of jury candidates, your lawyer group will have to decide which persons will be most fair to your side of the case. Use the answers to the questions and anything else you observe about the candidates. Your teacher will tell you how many candidates you can remove.

2. **Object to improper questioning.** Listen carefully to the questions of the opposing lawyer. You may *object* if you think something the opposing lawyer is doing or saying is unfair because it is: NOT RELEVANT
   LEADING (review page 55)
   HEARSAY (review page 59)
   BROWBEATING

   If you are asking questions and the other lawyer objects, listen to the objection, then tell the judge why your question should be allowed. If the judge does not allow the question, try to ask another question which will bring out the same facts.

3. **More questions for cross-examination.** Listen carefully when the witnesses for the other side testify. You may want to ask questions on cross-examination about something the witness says. Remember, your aim in cross-examination is:

   to get the witness to admit some fact which will help your side, or
   to show the witness is lying, or is unsure or confused about his/her testimony.

4. **Introduce physical evidence.** If you have any physical evidence, make sure you introduce it while the witness who can identify it is on the stand. Make sure you let the other side see the evidence so they can object if they think the evidence is not genuine or not relevant.

5. **Motion to dismiss.** (Defendant's lawyer) After all of the plaintiff's (or prosecution) witnesses have testified, the defendant's lawyer can ask the judge to dismiss the case. Do this only if you think the plaintiff's (or prosecution) evidence is so weak that you don't even have to present your evidence. If the judge agrees to dismiss, you win the case, but you don't get to call your witnesses.

THE JUDGE AND THE COURT REPORTER

INFORMATION FOR THE JUDGE

Your job is to act somewhat like a referee during the trial. You will need to be prepared to do the following things:

Rule on Objections. It is your job to decide whether to sustain or overrule objections made by the lawyers. Review what it means to sustain or overrule objections (pages 61 and 62). You might also want to review what kinds of questions are not proper. It will be helpful to write down some examples of proper and improper questions before the trial. Keep the list with you at the trial to help you decide whether a question to which a lawyer objects is proper or improper.

To help you decide whether a question asks for relevant facts, review the case summary before the trial and listen carefully to the opening statements so you know what the case is about.

When a lawyer makes an objection, ask him or her to state the reason for the objection. Ask the lawyer who posed the question to state why the question is proper. Then, make your ruling.

Rule on Motion to Dismiss. At the end of the plaintiff's evidence, the defendant's lawyer might ask you to dismiss the case. You will need to listen carefully to all of the evidence so you will know how to decide. You should only dismiss the case if you think that the plaintiff's evidence does not prove the plaintiff's side of the case even without the defendant's evidence to weaken it. If you overrule the motion ask the defendant's lawyer to begin questioning his/her witnesses.

Instruct the Jury. At the conclusion of the trial, when all the evidence has been presented, it is your job to instruct the jury. It is very important for you to give the instructions carefully so the jury will understand what the law requires them to decide. Read carefully the "Judge's Instructions to the Jury," (page 108 for civil trial or page 118 for criminal trial). You should understand the points of law in these instructions. Perhaps your teacher or a law student can help you.

Order in the Courtroom. During the trial, it will be your job to keep order in the courtroom. Do not let things get out of hand. You should also tell witnesses or lawyers to speak up if the jury can't hear them.

Read through Court Procedure (pages 105–111 for civil trial or pages 116–120 for criminal trial). Make certain you understand the words you will say during the trial and that you know when to say them.

INFORMATION FOR THE COURT REPORTER

Your job is to take down what the witnesses, lawyers and the judge say during the trial. Read carefully pages 67–70 so that you understand the duties of a court reporter.

Of course you won't have the use of the kind of machine which a court reporter would use but you could make up your own "shorthand code" to use during the trial. For example, "P. accid-11:20 p.m.," could mean that the plaintiff (P) testified that the accident happened at 11:20 p.m. Try to concentrate on the main points of each question and answer. Before the trial, read the case summary and depositions so that you are familiar with the names and terms that will come up during the trial. Practice your own shorthand code before the trial begins. It might also be helpful to go over the code you plan to use with the judge before the trial.

As a backup to your shorthand, you might want to use a tape recorder during the trial. Many student court reporters do this in mock trials so they can double-check on things they were not certain of during the trial. If you are able to locate a tape recorder, make sure you know how to use it.

5

THE CLERK AND THE BAILIFF

INFORMATION FOR THE CLERK

It is your job to make sure that the trial runs smoothly. To be prepared you might want to:

Reread Court Procedure for a Civil Trial, pages 105 to 110. Be aware of what is supposed to happen at each step of the trial. It is your job to swear in the witnesses. The oath "Do you swear to tell the truth, the whole truth, and nothing but the truth in this case under penalty of perjury, so help you God?" is repeated for each witness.

Make up your own subpoenas. They could be like this model. Perhaps your teacher will let you use a ditto master.

SUBPOENA

_____ COURTS

STATE OF _____

TO _____, GREETINGS;

You are hereby commanded, all excuses and delays set aside, that you be and appear before the Honorable Judge of the _____ Court in _____, on the _____ day of _____, A.D., 19___, at _____ a.m., then and there to testify and the truth of your knowledge to speak of and concerning a certain matter of controversy, in said Court now pending, wherein _____ is Plaintiff and _____ is Defendant, and this you shall in no wise omit, under legal penalty.

Witness, _____,
Clerk of our said Court, with seal thereof hereto affixed, at office in _____, this _____ day of _____, A.D., 19___.

Find out the names of the witnesses from the lawyers. Make up a subpoena for each witness. In a civil case the plaintiff and the defendant don't need subpoenas. Give the subpoenas to the bailiff to deliver to each of the witnesses in person. Prepare a list of witnesses, including the plaintiff and defendant, for the judge.

Prepare tags to use if, during the trial, you may be asked to mark physical evidence. The tags will be attached to the pieces of evidence (exhibits). When you mark the exhibit make sure you write down whose exhibit it is.

"Plaintiff's exhibit #_____"
"Defendant's exhibit #_____"

Do not mark any exhibits before the trial begins.

The clerk and the bailiff together plan how to arrange the school room to look like a courtroom. Think about items needed for the trial—a gavel, a robe for the judge, a bible, a clock or watch (to keep track of time). Decide where the various participants should sit during the trial. Make certain you have enough chairs, desks, tables.

INFORMATION FOR THE BAILIFF

You are in charge of the jury. During the trial you lead the jurors in and out of the courtroom at the correct times. (The jurors should be lined up in alphabetical order.) While the jury is deciding the case, you will be responsible for seeing that none of the jurors talk with any outsiders.

Before the trial begins you will get the subpoenas from the clerk. It is your job to deliver them to the witnesses and to the defendant in a criminal trial.

Reread the section Court Procedure for a Civil Trial, pages 105 to 110.

Make certain there is order in the courtroom during the trial. If anyone is talking loudly, walk over to that person and quietly tell him/her to be quiet.

Help the clerk plan how the classroom will be set up to look like a courtroom and get the props needed for the trial.

Before the trial begins, make a chart like the one below. There should be as many lines for names as there are students in the jury. Fill in the names of the students in alphabetical order. Ask each of them to tell you his/her age. Make a copy of this chart for each of the lawyers. When the lawyers have finished the voir dire, they will announce the names of the persons who will not be on the jury. Lead these students out of the jury area to another part of the room.

NAMES	ADDRESS	AGE	OCCUPATION
1.			
2.			
3.			
4.			
5.			
6.			
7.			
8.			
9.			
10.			
11.			

INFORMATION FOR JURY CANDIDATES

Your job is to make a fair decision in the case, based on the evidence presented at the trial.

Review Lesson 16. Make sure you understand voir dire and a juror's duty. The members of the jury will not be chosen officially until the voir dire at the beginning of the trial. However, all students in the jury group should take part in the following group work.

Select a jury foreperson. The foreperson is responsible for reviewing the judge's instructions with the other members of the jury. He/she also helps move the discussion along in the jury room when the jury is trying to reach a verdict. The foreperson reads the verdict in court.

During the trial, it is the duty of each juror to listen carefully to everything that is said. To practice your listening skills, do the following activity:

> Divide into groups of 3. One person in the group will be the "witness", one the "lawyer" and one the "jury." Then the "lawyer" will ask the "witness" questions about a particular book, TV show, or song. When the questions and answers are finished, the "jury" should try to repeat as many facts as possible. Do this activity two more times, changing parts so that each member of the group has a chance to play each part.

From this activity, what do you think of your ability to listen and understand?

It will be your job to decide which facts are true, which witnesses to believe. How do you make such a decision?

Working alone, read the testimony of each of the following witnesses. Decide which of them you believe. Think about the reasons for believing that witness.

Witnesses	Which witness do you believe?	Why?	Do you think your reasons for believing this witness are fair and reliable?
a. Alice is a very pretty woman who appears in court in fashionable clothes. She looks "very upper class". Tony appears in court in clothes which are obviously old. He is wearing a loud shirt and badly fitting trousers.			
b. Wong testifies that he paid the bill in full. The Dandy Store owner testifies that Wong paid a deposit but never paid the full bill. Wong's lawyer puts into evidence a check for the full amount from Wong to the Dandy Store and cashed by Mr. Dandy.			

Witnesses	Which witness do you believe?	Why?	Do you think your reasons for believing this witness are fair and reliable?
c. Eugenia testifies that she should not be responsible for the condition of the apartment because it was terrible when she moved in. The landlady testifies that the apartment is in terrible condition now because of what Eugenia did to it. Felipe, a neighbor, says he saw several holes in the walls before Eugenia moved in. Gladys testifies that she helped Eugenia move in and she noticed broken windows.			
d. Yolanda never raises her eyes while she testifies. She hestitates before she answers and then blurts out an answer quickly, as if she had memorized it. Ali looks at the lawyer and jury as he testifies. He answers questions as if he were having a conversation.			

Witnesses	Which witness do you believe?	Why?	Do you think your reasons for believing this witness are fair and reliable?
e. Bertha testifies that she did a good job building the fence for O'Henry. O'Henry testifies the fence is falling down because it was put up so poorly. Bertha's friend, Jerry, testifies that Bertha put up the fence the way everyone else does it. Lee, another fence installer, testifies that Bertha didn't put the fence deep enough into the ground.			

Discuss the reasons for believing a witness with the entire jury group. What other things might make you believe one witness more than another? Will your decision in the case be fair if you use those reasons to decide which witness is telling the truth? Why? Why not?

Note to teacher: Here is a community involvement project which is a beneficial and major undertaking. We placed this idea at the end of the book for you to give you the opportunity to decide if this is a project you think your students could do and benefit from. Often the instruction books that are given to jurors are not very interesting, are outdated, and are difficult to read. Students might do or redo a booklet for jurors that could be used by the courts. In doing the book, students would review much of the information learned in *Courts and Trials*, Second Edition. The project could also provide the students with a good reason to use and improve their language arts skills. It is a worthwhile project that could benefit the entire community.

If your courts have a jury booklet, the students should look at it for style and types of information. The booklet might include:

1. how the jury selection process works
2. the difference between civil and criminal cases
3. the court system with charts
4. explanation of voir dire
5. the oath of a juror
6. an outline of what happens in the trial including:
   a. opening statements
   b. witnesses and evidence
   c. examination of witnesses
   d. arguments
   e. instructions to the jury
7. how jurors should conduct themselves in the courtroom and during recess. Note that if jurors can't see or hear evidence or testimony, they should tell the judge.
8. conduct of jury in the jury room

A lawyer or law student should look at the students' booklet before it is sent to the jury commissioner or chief clerk. If they are interested, they might print it for use or ask you to find a group that would sponsor the printing of it. If you are working with students who are really enthusiastic about this, you might have the class ask a judge to write a short introduction for your booklet.